CK,

　　To the best bird photographer (& rescuer) I know! Enjoy the book & the bird hunts.

♡

Carol

Parking Lot Birding

NUMBER SIXTY

W. L. Moody Jr. Natural History Series

Parking Lot Birding

A FUN GUIDE TO DISCOVERING BIRDS IN TEXAS

Jennifer L. Bristol

Foreword by Richard Louv

TEXAS A&M UNIVERSITY PRESS | COLLEGE STATION

This paper meets the requirements
of ANSI/NISO Z39.48–1992 (Permanence of Paper).
Binding materials have been chosen for durability.
Manufactured in China through FCI Print Group.

Library of Congress Cataloging-in-Publication Data

Names: Bristol, Jennifer L., 1971– author.

Title: Parking lot birding : a fun guide to discovering birds in Texas / Jennifer L. Bristol.

Other titles: W.L. Moody Jr. natural history series ; no. 60.

Description: First edition. | College Station : Texas A&M University Press,

   [2020] | Series: W.L. Moody Jr. natural history series ; number 60 |

   Includes bibliographical references and index.

Identifiers: LCCN 2019044461 | ISBN 9781623498511 | ISBN 9781623498528 (ebook)

Subjects: LCSH: Birding sites—Texas—Guidebooks. | Bird

   watching—Texas—Guidebooks. | Recreation area parking

   facilities—Texas—Guidebooks.

Classification: LCC QL684.T4 B75 2020 | DDC 598.072/34764—dc23

LC record available at https://lccn.loc.gov/2019044461

Dedication

In memory
of Toody Byrd,
who inspired me to write

Dedicated to
the Scott Free Family Birding Team:
Thomas Nilles and Valarie Bristol
and
Evelyn Bristol; Walter Bristol;
and my grandmother, Martha Scott,
who always shared her love for
adventure, nature, and beauty

Contents

Foreword

It's hard to deny that Texas is big. With 268,596 square miles of ecological wonderment, it is second only to California in biodiversity. It stretches more than eight hundred miles from north to south and roughly the same east to west. In the vast expanse reside beaches, coastal prairies, lush pine forests, limestone-laden hill country, rolling blackland prairies, subtropical scrub country, desert, towering mountains, and birds. Texas is big on birds and is big on birding.

Texas can boast one of the greatest bird diversities of any state with more than six hundred species either living in or passing through as they migrate. The Central Flyway stretches across the state from north to south, while the Mississippi Flyway skirts along the Texas coastal region; both support a massive passage of birds, butterflies, and bats each spring and fall.

Nature tourism is also big in Texas, and birding is the cornerstone of that industry. Bird watching is one way people of all ages and from all walks of life can enjoy meaningful outdoor experiences without having to make a major time commitment or physical effort. Nature centers and parks provide children and families spaces to learn about and interact with nature in a safe, manageable setting. While national parks have prestige and allure, it is often the local parks that provide us with a sense of place as we form our first, and often strongest, bonds with nature.

In a state that has only 5 percent public lands and one of the fastest-growing populations in the country, nature centers, public lands, and the habitats they protect are an important piece of the conservation puzzle. They are also an integral part of our own health and well-being.

This book offers a guide to some of the best birding spots in Texas that are accessible to all people regardless of ability or mobility. Because adventures happen while exploring in the outdoors, Jennifer Bristol shares some of her family's stories as they romp across Texas. Moreover, she shares her sense of awe and wonder for nature and reverence for the rich cultural history of her home state.

Jennifer infuses her personal experiences and observations with research to succinctly describe what to expect from each of the more than one hundred stops. She is candid about what birds might be seen from the parking lot while also sparking the reader's curiosity to venture a little deeper into the woods, to visit the bird blind, stroll down the boardwalk, or ease on down the trail.

There is never any guarantee of what you might see when exploring in nature, especially in a state as big and ecologically diverse as Texas. However, one thing is for sure: you'll never know unless you step out the door and go.

—Richard Louv

Acknowledgments

This book would not have been possible without the love and support of my husband, Thomas Nilles, and his wonderful photography. Thomas and my mother, Valarie Bristol, are the core of the Scott Free Family Birding Team and have spent countless hours crisscrossing the state of Texas with me in search of birds. I also acknowledge my father, George Bristol, for his tireless efforts to conserve habitat in Texas and for influencing policies that support our national, state, and local public lands.

I thank all the amazing people I work with who support the vision that all children and their families deserve safe, equitable access to nature: Carter Smith, Nancy Herron, Hayden Brooks, Margaret Russell, Louie Bond, Darcy Bontempo, Brent Leisure, Shelly Plante, and many more—you inspire me. My deepest gratitude for Richard Louv, cofounder of the Children & Nature Network, for all his kind words of encouragement and beautiful foreword for the book. Jonathan Ogren and Karina Gonzalez at Siglo Group, thank you for your excellent maps. I send a special shout-out to the directors and staff of the nature centers and parks who work tirelessly to care for the wild places and wild things of Texas. Thanks also go to the keepers of the hawk watch towers and the volunteers who fill the bird feeders and keep the bird blinds clean.

Special thanks go to Barry Lands, Lisa Tanner, and all the Rocking B Riders for being willing to stop our trail rides to look at birds. Haven Lindsey, my gratitude for your editing and suggestions. I also thank my neighbors Ben and Linda Taylor for helping us actualize a dream of buying the land behind our homes to have our own private wildlife sanctuary and my uncle Steve and aunt Judy for brokering the land deal.

I send love to the ladies of Texas Women in Conservation. Susie Temple, I couldn't have done this without your years of encouragement to write and tell the story of nature. Mark Bristol, Jennifer C. Bristol, Evelyn Bristol, Walter Bristol, Jimmy Bristol, the cousins, and extended Bristol, Scott, Holt, and Nilles families—you rock.

Parking Lot Birding

Introduction

FIGURE I.1. Scott's Oriole on ocotillo in parking lot of Big Bend National Park (photo by Jennifer L. Bristol).

Birding has not always been a lifelong passion of mine. In fact, I arrived at the party rather late. And unlike many birders, I was not wowed by the activity right away. For most of my life I spent my time in nature racing headlong down mountain trails, swimming in every body of water I came across, and riding horses deep into the woods.

It was actually a horse to blame, or thank, for my transformation into a birding enthusiast. I was bucked off my mustang, Ranger, on a trail ride one hot September morning. I watched Ranger's back hooves barely clear my head as I landed flat on my back in the middle of a grassy field. (Yes, Mom, I was wearing my helmet!) The incident left me with a serious back injury and a deeply wounded ego.

The recovery took longer than a day, so naturally I grew frustrated, impatient, and a little down. My husband tried to cheer me up with activities and encouragement. In a last-ditch effort to get me out of my funk, he took me on a "photo safari" around

Austin. Occasionally, we would go on photo safaris to explore ghost towns of Texas or take pictures of wildflowers. On this trip, birds caught my attention and filled the lens of my camera with beautiful images.

My curiosity was sparked. I wanted to know the names of the birds I was seeing. I wanted to hear their songs and understand their habits. Nature was the elixir I needed to rebound from my physical and mental injury. And I soon craved more. The slow pace of birding didn't always agree with me, but the immersion in nature did. It wasn't long before most of our fall and spring trips revolved around birding.

Years earlier, my mother had made many attempts to get me interested in bird-watching, so naturally she was excited when I finally stumbled into the pursuit. She had a deep passion for birds and had dedicated most of her career as county com-missioner and director of the Trust for Public Lands and volunteer time with Travis Audubon securing conservation lands to protect critical bird habitat. In birding, habitat matters. But we'll get to that later.

Even as excited as I was about my new hobby, it lacked a little something. Then I began working for Texas Parks and Wildlife as the coordinator for the Texas Children in Nature program, and it was there that I was introduced to the Great Texas Birding Classic. Really? A birding competition? Be still, my overly competitive heart!

Some people competing for the first time might start off with a day event such as a "Big Sit" or a "Sunrise to Noon" competition. But not me. I talked my husband, mother, and an uncle into competing in the "Week Long Statewide" category. This particular category meant we would bird for six solid days anywhere in Texas and count as many species as we could find. Our first year we struggled to break 150 species, but we had a blast every step of the way.

In those first few years of competing, we took a lot of steps. We hiked deep into the hinterlands of national wildlife refuges along the Rio Grande. We walked softly into the Lost Pines of Bastrop State Park, and we struggled up and down the rocky trails of Central Texas. Mile after mile, year after year, we searched for birds as far from any human-made structures as we could. With each step we convinced ourselves that the birds would be just over the next hill or just around the next corner. We had some success, but in this mode we never got past third place in the Birding Classic.

To be honest, I was too stubborn to realize what is so glaringly obvious to many other birders: in most cases, the best birding happens at, or close to, the parking lot at a park, bird blind, boardwalk, or nature center. I didn't want to believe it—my ego wouldn't allow it. Perhaps due to my competitive nature and my willingness to traipse up, down, and around any obstacle far away from human-made structures, the parking lot reality offended my sense of awe and wonder for nature. I consider most parking lots, and the cars they keep, to be little more than a necessary evil.

As a child and later as an adult, I spent years observing wildlife in Montana's Glacier National Park and Flathead National Forest. In order to see grizzly bears, mountain goats, wolverines, and bighorn sheep, I hiked for miles along rocky alpine trails. Those observations were pure. They were earned. They felt special.

But in reality, it makes sense that it is easier to see more birds near a parking area or the campus of a nature center. Those cleared spaces make it easier to peer into the thickets, woods, wetlands, or fields that stretch out beyond the manicured areas that provide the necessary habitat the birds need. It's not that the birds prefer those spaces; it's just easier to see them from a contrived vantage point.

According to John Davis, director of the Wildlife Diversity Program at Texas Parks and Wildlife Department, "Satisfying wildlife experiences can be found all around us if we only look. While wilderness or intact ecosystems are most definitely needed for wildlife to thrive, we don't have to trek arduously into the hinterlands to have meaningful wildlife encounters. It's often the everyday, personal interactions that instill in us a deep connection to wildlife and nature."

This concept started to become a reality in my mind after my husband and I hiked the five-mile Wolf Mountain Trail at Pedernales Falls State Park. On that particularly hot spring day we were searching for the endangered Golden-cheeked Warbler. On our journey we frequently heard the bird calling but never caught a glimpse. The Texas sun was beating down on my fair skin and setting fire to my patience as we worked to find the elusive bird. As we approached the trailhead to return to our car without finding what we had hoped to discover, we noticed a stately woman peering silently through her binoculars. She looked cool and refreshed as she relaxed in the shade. "See much today?" I inquired.

"Oh, the male Golden-cheeked has been sitting right here for about an hour, just singing away," she replied in her cool southern voice.

Click, click, click. We snapped a few photos, had a few laughs, and drove home to Austin. For a few weeks, I stewed over the idea that this elusive bird was not where I had envisioned it being, and then I made my peace with it. It's fine to hike deep into the woods to spot a grizzly bear, but I began to understand that the lofty birds are more tolerant of sharing their habitat with ground dwellers such as humans.

This book in no way advocates for more parking lots. The reality is that it is simply easier to see the birds near a parking area, nature center, or bird blind or from a short raised boardwalk trail because those controlled spaces offer a vantage point where you can peer into the surrounding habitat. But the habitat that stretches beyond those minimized human activity areas is essential for birds and other wildlife. The miles of conservation lands, both public and private, are critical for wildlife to raise their families, feed, and live. Habitat matters.

Golden-cheeked Warblers will nest and breed only in the Ashe juniper– and live oak–filled canyons of the Texas Hill Country. Whooping Cranes must be able to find blue crabs in San Antonio Bay. Meadowlarks need stretches of prairies filled with native grasses and insects. Northern Bobwhites require undisturbed brush country.

Bald Eagles need tall trees near bodies of water with plenty of fish in them. Every species plays a role in the delicate balance of nature. The more we know about each of those roles, the better we are able to conserve lands and critical habitat for every species.

According to research conducted by the Cornell Lab of Ornithology only 10 percent of the habitat needed to support the migratory birds of North America is protected, and habitat loss is the number-one threat to migratory and resident birds. If that is so, then it becomes important to support organizations that endeavor to set aside conservation properties and work with private landowners to manage their lands with best practices that allow the birds and other wildlife to flourish.

While a bird feeder and a water feature might bring the birds into a nature center or backyard, it is no replacement for the seeds of a native plant or the fresh waters of a crystal-clear creek. You might even see flocks of birds year-round deep in the concrete jungles of a big city, but chances are they are not native to North America. Pigeons, House Sparrows, and European Starlings are all hardy urban birds that were brought to North America from Europe. They do not migrate because they are not following their ancestral life patterns. Large flocks of nonmigrating Great-tailed Grackles can be found now in most Texas urban areas; however, they are native to the Americas.

My intention for this book is to inspire you to explore Texas and see for yourself the amazing birds that live here and pass through the state on their migration. I find pleasure in birding near urban areas almost as much as in the most remote parts of Texas. Thankfully, we live in a state that offers wildlife-watching opportunities in or near every large urban center, making it easy to grab the binoculars and head out for a few hours when the weather and bird forecasts are just right.

I've broken the parking lot birding stops into nine regions that are centered on a large urban area or defined ecoregion. At each stop you will find the name and address, number of species that have been recorded, and types of birding amenities offered at the location.

Regions

Houston/Galveston
Piney Woods
Dallas/Fort Worth
Austin and Central Texas
San Antonio and Western Edwards Plateau
Corpus Christi and the Coastal Bend
Rio Grande Valley
Trans-Pecos
Lubbock and the Panhandle

Types of Birding Amenities

Parking lot
Nature center campus
Wastewater treatment facility
Campground
Short trail
Boardwalk
Bird blind
Observation platform
Driving tour
Tram tour
Ferry ride

About the Species Lists

The number of species listed after the name of the location comes from the counts recorded on the website eBird.com, which is operated by the Audubon Society and the Cornell Lab of Ornithology. I use eBird to record my sightings and have used the data collected on the website as research for this book. I chose to use the species counts from eBird because they are consistent across locations. I will note that the eBird lists might not have historical data; however, they have plenty of information about what is being seen on a daily basis for the past few years.

FIGURE 1.2. Male Indigo Bunting in bottlebrush (photo by Jennifer L. Bristol).

Additionally, I use the website and app iNaturalist to record birds, other wildlife, and plant observations when I am in the field and have the time. I also take the time to chat with nature center directors, biologists, fellow birders, and other naturalists to gather information about the habits of birds and migration patterns. I am not a biologist, just an avid naturalist who loves to explore the wild places of Texas.

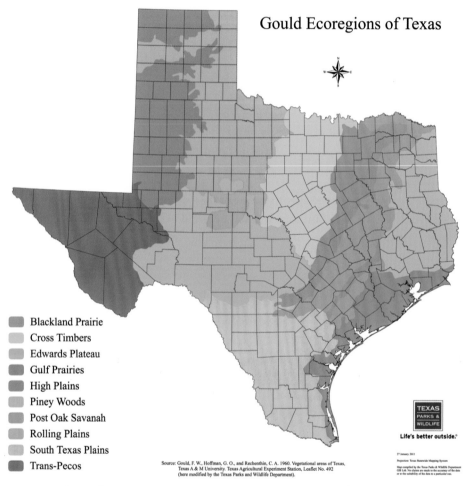

Gould Ecoregions of Texas

- Blackland Prairie
- Cross Timbers
- Edwards Plateau
- Gulf Prairies
- High Plains
- Piney Woods
- Post Oak Savanah
- Rolling Plains
- South Texas Plains
- Trans-Pecos

Source: Gould, F. W., Hoffman, G. O., and Rechenthin, C. A. 1960. Vegetational areas of Texas, Texas A & M University. Texas Agricultural Experiment Station, Leaflet No. 492 (here modified by the Texas Parks and Wildlife Department).

TEXAS
PARKS &
WILDLIFE

Life's better outside.®

Ecoregions of Texas (map courtesy of Texas Parks and Wildlife Department).

1 • Things to Know Before You Go

FIGURE 1.1. Verdin at Inks Lake State Park (photo by Jennifer L. Bristol).

Migratory Flyways, Highways of the Sky

Texas is the gateway for migratory birds as they pass from Central and South America into North America. Texas is the heart of the Central Flyway, with overlap in South and East Texas with the Mississippi Flyway; both are super-highways for hundreds of migrating bird species as well as bats, moths, and butterflies. Once the birds cross the Gulf of Mexico or journey through the mountains and plains of Central America, they can travel along the Great Plains, the longest piece of land uninhibited by mountains in the world.

Every spring and fall the Central and Mississippi Flyways are a frenzy of bird activity along the Rio Grande Valley and Gulf Coast. The Mississippi Flyway continues through the South Texas Plains and Gulf Coast Prairies and Marshes into the Piney

Woods of East Texas before continuing into Louisiana and along the Mississippi watershed. Not all birds are willing to make the dangerous journey across the Gulf of Mexico and prefer to glide over solid earth as they follow the eternal summer.

For centuries, the Great Plains have offered birds a source of food via freshwater fish, seeds, berries, and insects, in addition to water and shelter as they made their annual journeys. Like many places in the world, the habitat of the Great Plains has changed in recent history as a result of agriculture and human habitation. Birds can't shop at Walmart for food; they need native plants and insects that bloom and emerge in nature's carefully orchestrated symphony.

For many birds, insects are the primary source of food. Not just any bug will do. Each bird species has evolved to eat a variety of insects at certain times of the year as they move along on their journey. Humans alter those insect populations as they spray to minimize impact to crops or try to eradicate pests from yards and homes. The balance is difficult, but thankfully new lessons and technologies develop every year to improve that delicate equilibrium. Famed naturalist Rachel Carson was one of the first to study and raise the alarm about the ill effects that chemicals used in pesticides and herbicides have on insect, fish, and bird populations in her book *Silent Spring*. The title itself evokes an emotional response in me as I think how sad it would be to wake up one year and not hear the songs and chatter of birds in spring.

Extreme weather caused by climate change negatively impacts birds as well. Tornados, hurricanes, and freak snowstorms are just some of the many hazards the birds must navigate as they struggle to survive and raise their families. Warmer springs can cause certain insects to emerge early, and the birds that are synchronized by nature to consume those insects when they are larvae or pupae may miss out on an important food source during their journey. Extreme weather also brings extreme drought, which is problematic for forests, as it leaves them more susceptible to killer beetles or blights and raging wildfires. Additionally, the wetlands that support so many wading birds and waterfowl continue to be filled in across the Americas, further chipping away critical habitat.

When I was the program director for Camp Fire Central Texas, I created an after-school lesson about bird migration. The kids had to pretend that they were a migrating flock of geese. To complete the journey, they had to avoid all the migration hazards along the way. Answering a question incorrectly could result in their being knocked out by extreme weather, taken down by a power line or glass building, starved in a drought, or caught up in a hurricane. If they answered the questions correctly, they lived, made friends, raised families, and vacationed in South America. The kids enjoyed the lifelike lesson, and by the end of the experience they were rooting for each other and for the survival of the team/flock. I found that anytime kids could relate to wildlife, they quickly learned to empathize with that species. In other words, kids who learn about nature tend to care about nature.

My goal is to help everyone access and connect with nature in ways that are fun, informative, and easy. Most of the recommended birding locations should be accessible for all people with all abilities. Because of my work, I have a special affinity for parents or grandparents trying to get kids outdoors to learn to notice, respect, and understand nature. I hope this book will be a resource to find local birding spots that both surprise and delight.

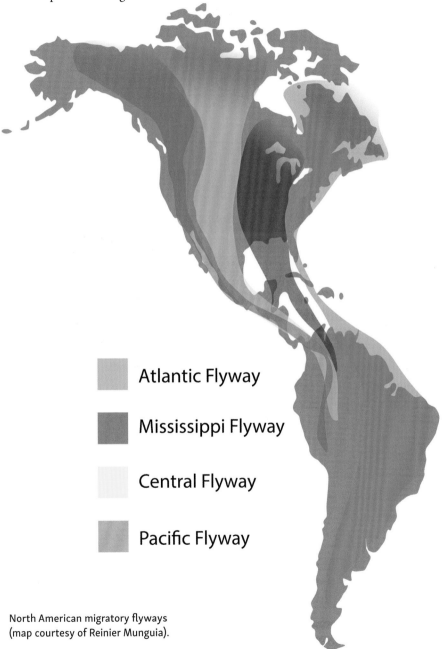

Atlantic Flyway

Mississippi Flyway

Central Flyway

Pacific Flyway

North American migratory flyways
(map courtesy of Reinier Munguia).

Birding and Conservation Ethics

I personally place an extremely high value on ethical birding and wildlife observation. It is important to remember that you are a predator in the eyes of all other wildlife. Even if you are a vegan, other types of wildlife don't know that you prefer carrots and kale to them and their young. When in the field, I practice the American Birding Association Code of Birding Ethics and all Leave No Trace principles. I want to enjoy wildlife in the wild and ensure that future generations have the same access to the animals I enjoyed as a child and now as an adult. I hope that you will also practice the ethics listed here and always err on the side of caution and respect when observing nature.

I will paraphrase what those codes and ethics are as the list is rather long. Basically, be respectful to wildlife and the habitats they depend on. In other words, don't stress the birds out by trying to get a perfect photo by climbing a tree to peer into their nest or trespass onto someone's private property to find a rare species. When at a park or nature center, walk only on designated trails to minimize impact on habitat and to avoid getting lost. Know your limits when you are out exploring, and make sure you plan ahead so you have enough water and food and a good map or powered-up cell phone if you plan on being out for a few hours.

If you do want to bring the birds into your yard, make sure feeders and water stations are clean. A feeder can also attract house cats and other predators, so consider the placement of the feeders to minimize unwanted encounters.

If you do witness someone being unethical or even questionable, speak up. Let a park ranger know if someone is doing something shady, or politely ask the person to voluntarily stop harassing wildlife or harming habitat. On multiple occasions I have encountered people in the pursuit of a perfect photo of a wild animal (even a grizzly bear), and I calmly reminded them that what they were doing was causing stress to the animal. Not everyone is comfortable with addressing a fellow citizen, but please take the time to report unethical and certainly unlawful behavior. Texas has some of the best park rangers and game wardens in the world. Remember that it is unlawful to collect live or dead species; take only photos, please.

You can also avoid putting undue stress on wildlife by talking in a soft, low voice and moving slowly when in close proximity to a bird or other species. That rule is hard for my family to follow, as we are all loud talkers, but we try our best.

Planning Your Trip

Like all outdoor adventures, a birding trip takes a little planning to ensure maximum enjoyment. I've done a lot of stupid things, from leaving all my gear at home to getting lost without a map while out of cell-phone service. Let my mistakes benefit you.

First, it's never fun to bird in the pouring rain, blinding heat, or hurricane-strength winds. Check the weather for the location you plan to visit, and make sure there isn't a fast-moving weather system that is forecast to arrive during your visit. In Texas, the weather can change in the blink of an eye, so practice a little "know before you go." There are all sorts of weather apps for your smartphone, and I strongly recommend installing one to be safe while in the field.

Second, make sure you don't pack your gear and leave it by the front door. Been there, done that. Take it with you! Also remember to charge your camera batteries the night before or pack an extra one so you don't miss out on a great shot. In my birding backpack I have my binoculars, camera, a lens cleaner, lightweight rain jacket, water bottle, small snack or a lunch depending on the day, small note pad and pen, battery charger for my camera, sunscreen, sunglasses, and of course, my lipstick. I live by my grandmother's creed that a good Texas girl should never be more than lunging distance from her lipstick at any given time.

A good pair of binoculars is worth every penny. There are lots of brands out there, but what is most important is to go to a sporting goods store and try a few pair. Let them dangle around your neck, hold them up to your face, and think about how they feel in your hands. Get a pair that is easy to hold and feels comfortable for your size and build. You might also want to talk to other birders in the field or read a few reviews online before making the investment.

Third, it's always a good idea to plug the address of the location you plan to visit into your phone or car GPS before heading out. Oftentimes if I am making multiple stops, I plug them all into my phone the night before. I also recommend having a backup birding location in case the first one doesn't work out or is closed for some reason. If you get off course, please pull your car off the road before engaging with your cell phone or navigation system. Even though our world is totally plugged in these days, it is always a good idea to take a paper map, especially if you are traveling into the wilds of West Texas.

Some locations listed are free to the public and open year-round, while others might charge an entrance fee or have limited hours. It's always a good idea to either call ahead to make sure they are open or check their hours online; each location in this book has a website listed. I also recommend getting a Texas State Parks Pass if you plan on visiting multiple state parks, and a National Parks pass is useful if you are planning a trip to far West Texas.

While this book focuses on birding, each location is also filled with other natural wonders and wildlife. I hope you will take the time to notice all the nature each location offers and even visit certain places in a variety of seasons to discover what gifts they reveal at different times of the year.

Safety Tips

By following the birding ethics and Leave No Trace principles, you will help ensure your safety and the safety of the birds. Following are a few additional tips to be safe.

Texas is a place of extreme weather and extreme nature. I highly recommend always lathering on sunscreen, wearing a hat, and drinking plenty of water while outdoors. Getting a blistering sunburn or becoming dehydrated is zero fun and can be dangerous.

Being on the coast for a fallout of birds is exciting; however, it also means the weather will change rapidly from a nice warm afternoon to a colder, windy day. To prepare, pack some layers of clothing, especially during the spring. Getting caught outdoors in a "Blue Norther" is also zero fun. A distant relative of mine was caught in a Blue Norther while tending his sheep near Santa Anna in the early 1900s. He caught pneumonia from the event and died within a few weeks. That story is one of the many life lessons my grandparents bestowed on my brother and me to ensure we were raised to be strong, responsible Texans. I used to think the lesson was to never raise sheep or live in Santa Anna but later learned it was about respecting the weather.

Texas is also home to a variety of plants that want nothing more than to make your life miserable. Get to know what poison ivy looks like, and remember: "leaves of three, let it be." When walking in the brush country or even the Hill Country, it's a good idea to wear lightweight long pants to avoid unwanted contact with thorny plants. Whatever you do, don't sit on a cactus. That's also zero fun.

Fire ants build small mounds that look like benign dirt piles. But beware; those little ants can unleash a world of hurt. Not all ants are bad, but fire ants are invasive and will swarm if you do not get off their mound quickly. Red ants are large ants that build their homes in the ground and make a big circle around the single hole that leads into their lair. These ants are good and one of the primary food sources for horned lizards and quail.

I tend to avoid all snakes. Only a few snakes in Texas are venomous, but in the moment, when they slither by, I just assume they are all deadly and give them a wide berth.

If you plan on birding with your dog, make sure it is always on a leash and under your control, and pack extra water for it. Not all nature centers or parks allow dogs, so check their policies before you get there. And please, please, never leave your dog friend in a hot car even for a second. Walking around on hot pavement can also be dangerous for dogs, as it burns the pads of their feet. I take my dogs birding with me only during the cooler months; however, they do make it difficult to take a good photo when I am trying to focus the lens and they are pulling on the leash.

Birding with Limited Mobility

When possible, I try to note if a birding stop has trails that can be easily enjoyed by people using a mobility device or traveling with children in strollers. Most nature centers and national and state parks make at least a portion of their trails ADA (Americans with Disabilities Act) accessible. Most boardwalks and observation decks are also ADA accessible. Thankfully, most of the birding spots I mention are located in terrain that is flat, which makes walking or wheeling around easier.

Birding by Sound

I personally don't have the best vision and require lots of optics to bring the birds into focus. I do, however, have good hearing and taught myself to bird by sound to identify a good number of species. Birding by sound takes a little longer to master but is worth it, especially in regions where the forests or vegetation is thick. There are several apps that can help you learn the various songs of migrating and local birds. It does take a moment to retrain your brain to listen intently to the conversation of nature. Birds have songs, tweets, and chatter that they use to communicate a wealth of knowledge.

Listening to birds is the same as listening to music. For example, Willie Nelson has a very different voice from George Strait's. Dolly Parton sounds different from Beyoncé. Prince has a whole different range than Billy Idol does. Once you start thinking about

FIGURE 1.2. Bird blind ahead (photo by Jennifer L. Bristol).

each species as having a voice that is different from the others, things will start to fall into place for learning their songs and sounds.

Start with the common birds around your home or favorite park, and see if you can add at least one bird each time you venture out. But remember that it is unethical to play a bird song to lure birds in so you can see them better. If you are verifying the sound, please play it at a level at which you can hear it but one that won't disturb the birds, especially during mating season.

Let's go birding!

2 • Houston/Galveston

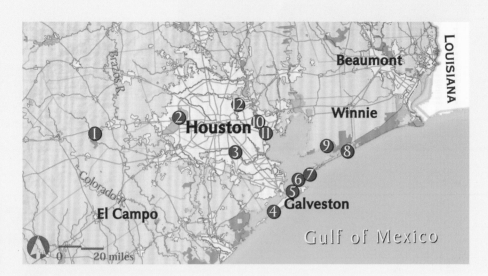

HOUSTON/GALVESTON REGION

KEY:

1   Attwater Prairie Chicken National Wildlife Refuge
2   Bear Creek Pioneers Park
3   El Franco Lee Park
4   Lafitte's Cove Nature Preserve
5   Bolivar Peninsula: Galveston Ferry Landing
6   Bolivar Peninsula: Frenchtown Road and Horseshoe Marsh Bird Sanctuary
7   Bolivar Flats Shorebird Sanctuary
8   High Island: Boy Scout Woods
9   Anahuac National Wildlife Refuge
10 Baytown Nature Center
11 San Jacinto Battleground State Historic Site
12 Sheldon Lake State Park and Environmental Learning Center

FIGURE 2.1. Great Egret and Reddish Egret (photo by Jennifer L. Bristol).

FIGURE 2.2. Gulls, skimmers, and terns on Bolivar Peninsula (photo by Jennifer L. Bristol).

FIGURE 2.3. Common Yellowthroat (photo by Jennifer L. Bristol).

Houston/Galveston metro region sits at the northern reach of what Texas Parks and Wildlife Department defines as the Gulf Prairies and Marshes, which extends along the 360 miles of Texas coastline. The conservation organization Houston Wilderness states that the region is "situated in one of the most ecologically diverse major urban areas in the country. The forests, prairies, savannahs, bayous, bottomlands, coastlines, and ocean around Houston and Galveston is comprised of ten eco-regions: seven land-based and three water-based." The organization is also quick to point out that the region has more biodiversity than any other part of the state. The variety of habitat makes it a wonderland for exploring nature and birding year-round.

While all of this is true, the region is also home to the fourth-largest city in the United States, second-busiest port per tonnage, and most of the major oil companies in the world. The port of Houston alone sprawls over twenty-five miles and is rimmed with a dizzying number of chemical plants, refineries, and businesses related to the transportation industry. It is also rich with human history from Native Americans who lived and hunted the region, to the battle for Texas Independence, to the exploration of space. The intense human population makes each natural place feel important and valuable.

The flooding that occurred during Hurricane Harvey in 2017 highlighted the need to protect the region's prairies and upstream bottomlands that help absorb the intense rains. As a result, hopefully more conservation lands or easements will be set aside to mitigate the impact of such extreme weather on the citizens, birds, and other wildlife of the area. Whether you are birding the bayous, prairies, or forests or near the beach, there is a lot of nature to discover in the Houston/Galveston metro area.

Attwater Prairie Chicken National Wildlife Refuge (286 species)

1206 APCNWR Road, Eagle Lake, TX 77434
https://www.fws.gov/refuge/attwater_prairie_chicken/
Parking Lot, Short Walk, Bird Blind,
Observation Platform, Driving Tour

If you want to see Attwater's Prairie-Chickens, you have to be dedicated to getting up before dawn, driving to the refuge, and standing in the cool morning air for a chance to hear the males "booming" during breeding season. They are elusive, ground-dwelling birds that live in the tallgrass prairie of the coast but have amazing camouflage that helps them blend into the grasses. I personally have never seen or heard the endangered bird, but I have tried many times.

Don't worry if you don't see the Attwater's Prairie-Chicken at the refuge; there are hundreds of birds to keep your optics busy. I've spent a lot of time birding the parking lot, grounds, and fields surrounding the visitor center. It's an easy stop and a nice break in the I-10 rat race as I travel back and forth from Austin to Houston for work or for visits with friends. The visitor center has a good collection of birds on display, which helps with identifying and understanding what you might see at the refuge.

A short loop trail passes through the prairie to the wooded area along the San Bernard River and Coushatta Creek. The change in habitat from prairie to riparian allows an opportunity to see more than twenty species of sparrows, such as Chipping, Grasshopper, and LeConte's Sparrows feeding alongside Sprague's and American Pipits. From November to March keep your eyes on the lookout at Horseshoe Lake for Double-crested Cormorants, American Coots, Blue-winged and Cinnamon Teals, Gadwalls, and a number of wading birds. The small lake has an observation platform and trail that offer good views of the two islands in the middle that serve as rookeries in the spring. Because of the lake and wetlands the refuge hosts more than twenty-five species of waterfowl throughout the year, with most occurring from November to March.

The driving tour is also great, but be sure to drive slowly and keep your windows rolled down, unless the bugs are too thick. In the prairie it's easier to hear the birds, stop, and look in the direction of the sound than just search the area with your binoculars. The staff and volunteers at the refuge also offer a variety of excellent guided birding trips for all skill levels, and they even offer tours to take you out to look for the elusive Attwater's Prairie-Chickens.

During the winter months the wetlands and fields can fill with Snow and White-fronted Geese, White-tailed and Red-tailed Hawks, Northern Harriers, and even Sandhill Cranes. This location is a perfect example of why habitat matters. According to the US Fish and Wildlife Service, the Attwater's Prairie-Chicken once occupied around six million acres of coastal prairie habitat. By 1919 the population disappeared from Louisiana, and in 1937 hunting of the once-common tallgrass prairie grouse was discontinued. As urban and agricultural expansion continued, the prairies have been diminished to just two hundred thousand fragmented acres left to support the remaining birds. Exploring the wildlife refuge is a good way to understand the complexity of the prairie ecosystem and consider what the land must have looked like prior to being altered by humans.

≫ **Feather Fact** ≪

Attwater's Prairie-Chicken: The Attwater's Prairie-Chicken isn't actually a chicken but a grouse that once roamed the coastal prairies of Texas and Louisiana. Today it is considered one of the most endangered birds in North America, mostly because of habitat loss. During breeding season the males inflate their bright yellow air sacks to omit a "booming" sound while they quickly stomp their feet on the ground. They look fairly frantic while in this state, but apparently the females dig it.

FIGURE 2.4. Male Attwater's Prairie-Chicken booming (photo courtesy of Greg Lasley; used with permission).

Bear Creek Pioneers Park (264 species)

3535 War Memorial Drive, Houston, TX 77084
http://www.pct3.com/Parks/all-parks/bear-creek-park
Parking Lots, Short Trails

This park is rather large and has numerous picnic areas and parking lots. My husband and I have visited a few times and been impressed with the birding at several locations in the park. The intersection of Patterson Road and Bear Creek Drive is a little hotspot for sparrows, blackbirds, and flycatchers. On a pleasant day in January, we spotted Brewer's Blackbirds, Eastern Bluebirds, Chipping Sparrows, American Pipits, American Robins, and Northern Cardinals all in one great flock feeding along the grassy area. During the spring a different wave of ground feeders shows up, such as Gray-cheeked and Wood Thrushes and Northern Waterthrushes.

During the spring migration the trees fill with warblers and sparrows as they pass through. It takes a little more patience to bird here, as the forests are thick with a variety of tall trees and dense shrubs. Timing is everything if you want to see the migrants. I recommend picking a few days around the first of April to visit when the trees are not as thick with foliage and the weather isn't steamy hot yet. Of course, the fall is an even better time to bird, when the leaves are dropping; the male birds, though, are not in breeding colors.

Langham Creek, which runs behind most of the picnic areas of Golbow Drive, is a good place to find Great Blue and Green Herons, Yellow-crowned Night-Herons, Snowy Egrets, and White Ibises. The woods along the creek often attract Yellow-billed Cuckoos and Belted Kingfishers in addition to a variety of woodpeckers and fly-catchers. The ponds around the golf course area also bring in a variety of ducks and geese during the winter. If you are up for a nature walk, there are several trails that meander through the forest and along Bear Creek.

The large, 2,154-acre park doubles as a flood mitigation property called the Addicks Reservoir and often has standing water after a heavy rain, so take some bug spray when visiting. The Addicks Reservoir was constructed in 1945 by the Army Corps of Engineers to stop the flooding that repeatedly plagues the city. It is reported that when Europeans first settled the area in the mid-1800s, the Louisiana black bear was still common in the mix of piney woods and prairies, hence the name Bear Creek Park. But don't worry; there are no longer any wild black bears in or near the park. Since this stop is a rather large urban park with numerous parking lots to explore, I recommend making a few visits during various times of the year to really discover all it has to offer.

≫ Feather Fact ≪

Northern Cardinal: Do you ever think you are seeing the same vibrant red bird in your yard year after year? You probably are. These hardy birds can live up to fifteen years in the wild and are adaptable to most of the central and eastern parts of North America. They are abundant in all parts of Texas except in the far west. Their large beak serves them well since they are opportunistic feeders who dine on everything from snails to seeds to grapes. Males are known to fiercely defend their territory and will even fight their own reflection on shiny surfaces like windows or the rearview mirror of a car. A group of these striking birds is known as a conclave, college, or Vatican.

FIGURE 2.5. Male Northern Cardinal (photo by Jennifer L. Bristol).

El Franco Lee Park (291 species)
9400 Hall Road, Houston, TX 77089
http://hcp1.net/Parks/ElFrancoLee
Parking Lots, Short Trails, Bird Blinds, Observation Platform

This is a pretty traditional urban park operated by Harris County, complete with ball fields, playgrounds, and walking trails. The park has a shallow pond that attracts a variety of ducks, geese, and shorebirds, while the trees rimming the pond are frequented by warblers and blackbirds.

When you enter the park, you have loads of parking lot choices. I recommend driving to the last parking area on either side of the lake. The north shore has a short boardwalk and observation pavilion that juts out into the marshy side of the reservoir, making it easy to see White Ibises, Roseate Spoonbills, Great and Snowy Egrets, Great Blue and Little Blue Herons, and Greater Yellowlegs all mingling with Green-winged Teals, Black-bellied Whistling-Ducks, and Hooded Mergansers.

The south shore parking lot yields a bird blind and a small butterfly garden that attracts sparrows and seedeaters along with a lovely variety of butterflies and moths. This park really gets hopping during the spring migration. It is easy to focus on the lake as the main attraction; however, the fields and woods are where the majority of birds that visit this 360-acre park hang out. In April alone 194 species have been reported on eBird, including Black-and-white, Tennessee, and Yellow Warblers; Indigo Buntings; and Summer Tanagers.

There is a nice crushed-granite and partially paved walking trail that loops around the pond, which is approximately two miles in length. If you are up for it, I recommend taking the walk along the boardwalk or to one of the bird blinds. There are benches along the way where you can take a break and make observations. On a quick trip in January, my husband and I spotted thirty-five species in under an hour. I've also visited in June and found the birding to be great as I meandered along the shady parts of the trail on the eastern side of the pond.

This park is free and open to the public; pets are allowed as long as they are on leash and under the control of their owner. There are restrooms near the sports park area.

Great Egret: This elegant, large white wading bird can be found year-round in Texas' wetlands and along the coast. The Great Egret is larger than the Snowy Egret but smaller than the Great Blue Heron. During breeding season males develop a neon-green patch between their beak and eye, and they develop long plumes along their back that are used to dazzle the females. Human females also became enamored with these plumes during the Victorian era and used them to decorate their hats. Their populations have recovered and are stable after being hunted almost to extinction for the milliner trade at the turn of the nineteenth century.

FIGURE 2.6. Great Egret (photo by Jennifer L. Bristol).

Lafitte's Cove Nature Preserve (325 species)
3503 Eckert Drive, Galveston, TX 77554
https://www.galveston.com/lafittespreserve/
Boardwalk, Short Trail, Bird Blind

Set on a small ridge along the barrier island, this oak grove and the surrounding wetlands are a true migrant trap. There is not much to see from the small parking lot, but there is a nice pavilion to sit in at the end of the boardwalk and benches along the paved paths that wind through the thicket where you can sit and enjoy the parade of birds. I recommend making a lap around the trail and keeping your eyes focused on the canopy for warblers and orioles. This place comes alive in the spring and fall with migrating and even some rare species that show up from time to time. For example, I once spotted a Whiskered Vireo catching bugs along the tops of the hackberry trees.

Through my experience I offer a caution. Do not make the mistake my husband and I made by trying to buddy up to the camera jockeys that set up camp around the drips with their mega gear and will not move to allow novice birders like us to squeeze in and snap a photo. My sweet, chatterbox husband tried to strike up a conversation with one of the gear guys, and it ended with him receiving a decisive "shush." I started laughing uncontrollably and had to scamper down the trail so as not to draw more unwarranted shushing.

Aside from that, the birding is great. You will most likely experience "warbler neck" at this location. There are few ground birds in the woods, so for the most part the colorful avian friends dance about the treetops looking for insects or feasting on mustang grapes. However, when large flocks of Indigo Buntings arrive in the spring, they can be found in the grassy fields around the perimeter of the woods.

The wetlands near the parking lot offer a variety of shorebirds and ducks. I've spotted Whimbrels, Greater Yellowlegs, Roseate Spoonbills, Great Blue Herons, Blue-winged Teals, and Black-bellied Whistling-Ducks in the shallow ponds. The yards surrounding the large houses near the parking lot often attract White and White-faced Ibises.

Jean Lafitte was a pirate/privateer who helped establish Galveston as an important harbor and shipping route. History tells us that despite his moral flexibility, he was a brilliant captain who understood the waters of the Texas coast like no other commander of his time. He and his fleet helped General Andrew Jackson defend New Orleans in 1812 against the British. Soon after that battle he moved his fleet to the area around Galveston and set up a pirate's colony know as *Campeche*. His home and settlement existed close to where the ferry currently crosses from Galveston to the Bolivar Peninsula. The cove that bears his name was one of the places he stashed booty and hid his ships; there is a historical marker on the other side of the road near the entrance to the housing development.

≫ Feather Fact ≪

Indigo Bunting: This vibrant blue bird isn't actually blue at all. The blue light is refracted from tiny structures on the feathers to give them a jewel-like color. Indigo Buntings fly at night and navigate by the stars between South and North America. They nest in open woodlands, including parts of East Texas. They can often be seen in flocks foraging along the ground for seeds and insects. During the fall migration males are no longer in their breeding blue plumage and are a drab brown that can make them difficult to identify. Like Painted Buntings, these birds are often trapped to become part of the illegal pet trade.

FIGURE 2.7. Male Indigo Bunting (photo by Jennifer L. Bristol).

Bolivar Peninsula: Multiple Stops

This is shorebird central. My advice is to start early in the morning and ride the ferry from Galveston during the spring migration or during the winter when the shorebirds are hanging out. Riding the ferry is always fun as you watch the tanker ships and tugboats move slowly from the Gulf of Mexico into the ring of ports surrounding Galveston and Trinity Bays. My mother prefers going up to the observation deck, but I like the back of the boat to be up close and personal with the gulls, terns, and best of all, the Magnificent Frigatebirds. I personally think the Magnificent Frigatebird is one of the coolest birds in all of the Americas.

I almost suffered a full mutiny from my fellow birding team members when I woke them before dawn to bird the Bolivar Peninsula and High Island for fourteen hours straight. I plied them with fried food and vats of iced tea from the Stingaree Restaurant and Bar in Crystal Beach during the middle of the day to regroup and bolster their flagging enthusiasm. You don't have to bird the area for fourteen hours to have a great time and enjoy the wild spaces, but I do recommend not being in a rush and giving yourself plenty of time to explore the marshes and coast.

⫸ Feather Fact ⫷

Magnificent Frigatebird: Sometimes referred to as the "Man-O-War," this graceful flyer is designed perfectly to snatch a meal away from other gulls and terns with its long bill that has a sharp hook at the tip. It is easiest to see these birds from a ferry or boat when the gulls or terns are hunting for fish behind the vessel. Their long, thin wings and forked tail allow them to float on the sea breezes with minimal effort for hours, even days on end. Females have a white head and breast and are larger than the males. Males have a distinct red balloon-like pouch at the base of their neck that they inflate during breeding season to attract a mate. They are one of the few seabirds that rarely lands on the water. They can be found along the Texas coast from late spring to fall. During Hurricane Harvey six of these birds were spotted at Lake Walter E. Long Park in east Austin.

FIGURE 2.8. Female Magnificent Frigatebird (photo by Jennifer L. Bristol).

Bolivar Peninsula: Galveston Ferry Landing (189 species)
State Highway 87, Port Bolivar, TX 77650
https://www.galveston.com/galvestonferry
Parking Lot, Ferry Ride

Pelicans, cormorants, and other shorebirds are all present to greet visitors as soon as they dock at the ferry landing. I've also always had luck spotting Boat-tailed Grackles and Barn Swallows in the parking lot of the ferry landing. The report on eBird shows upward of two hundred species spotted from the Bolivar–Galveston Ferry parking lot. I also recommend stopping here for the restroom since there are none at the other locations along Bolivar.

⋙ Feather Fact ⋘

Laughing Gull: This bird and its joyful sound can be found along the beaches of the Gulf of Mexico and the Atlantic and Pacific Coasts of North and Central America. These seemingly common seabirds once saw their populations dwindle as their feathers became desirable for the hat trade in the early nineteenth century. Their eggs weakened and cracked as a result of the use of DDT and the popularization of driving along beaches. Thanks to conservation efforts this lofty seabird has made a strong recovery, especially along the Texas coastline. During times of low pressure gulls will settle down to roost, which is often a good sign that rain might be on the way.

FIGURE 2.9. Laughing Gulls in love (photo by Jennifer L. Bristol).

Bolivar Peninsula: Frenchtown Road and Horseshoe Marsh Bird Sanctuary (233 species)

Frenchtown Road and First Street, Bolivar, TX 77650
https://houstonaudubon.org/sanctuaries/bolivar-flats/horseshoe-marsh.html
Parking Lot

Leaving the ferry area, take a drive down Frenchtown Road to look for more shore-birds hanging out in the marshes. Your car acts as your bird blind on this adventure. From the road I've seen Soras, King Rails, Clapper Rails, Long-billed Curlews, and Tricolored Herons foraging in the grasses for fish, frogs, and invertebrates. The marshes fill with sparrows, blackbirds, ducks, and buntings while the ever-present Northern Harrier swoops in low over the grasses as it hunts for a lively treat. Follow Frenchtown Road until it becomes First Street and finally crosses Seventh Street and the 108 Loop that meanders through the Horseshoe Marsh Bird Sanctuary.

The Bolivar Peninsula offers a generous habitat mix of coastal prairies, freshwater and saltwater marshes, beaches, and dunes, which allows such a variety of birds to flourish in the region. However, the area is prone to flooding and is under constant threat of a disastrous oil spill from one of the refineries located along Galveston and Trinity Bays or tankers that sail along the Intracoastal Waterway. The Port of Houston is the second-busiest port in the United States and the sixteenth busiest in the world.

≫ **Feather Fact** ≪

Long-billed Curlew: The defining physical characteristic of North America's largest shorebird is its long, pink-and-black curved bill. Curlews use their sensitive bill to bore deep into the tidal mudflats for shrimp and other invertebrates or worms in the grasslands. They winter along the Gulf Coast, migrate through Texas, and nest in the Great Plains and Great Basin. This bird is also known as the "Candlestick Bird," which is what some believe gave Candlestick Point in San Francisco its name. Curlews are on the State of North American Birds Watch List as one of greatest concern because of loss of habitat and ill effects of pesticides on invertebrates and insects.

FIGURE 2.10. Long-billed Curlew on Frenchtown Road (photo by Jennifer L. Bristol).

Bolivar Flats Shorebird Sanctuary (313 species)
Rettilon Road, Bolivar, TX 77650
https://houstonaudubon.org/sanctuaries/bolivar-flats/
Parking Lot

As you turn away from the bay side of the peninsula, I recommend visiting the Bolivar Flats Shorebird Sanctuary, which is owned and managed by the Houston Audubon Society. This section of the island has been designated as a Globally Important Bird Area and an international site in the Western Hemisphere Shorebird Reserve Network. The network is a system of preserves that focus specifically on the conservation of wetlands and critical habitat where shorebirds nest or winter.

Mornings and evenings are the best times to visit the marshes, prairies, and seashores, although anytime is fine. Visitors can stop along the road to watch American Avocets twist and turn as they dance across the sky in unison from marsh to marsh. The fields can sometimes look devoid of life, but when you look closer, you will see flickers of movement in the clumps of grass or hear the trilling call of a Marsh Wren. Wrens, sparrows, and blackbirds all join the shorebirds and ducks in the mix of wetlands and sea grass fields. Lucky visitors who get up early might catch a glimpse of the hauntingly beautiful Barn Owl sitting in its house that rests atop a pole located halfway down Rettilon Road. The Barn Owl has also been sighted at the nearby water tower located off Frenchtown Road. Check eBird or ask other birders for recent sightings.

I suggest having either a truck or SUV to drive onto the beach and park at the edge of the shorebird survey area; a parking pass is required to park on the beach. The birding is great even if you venture only a few feet from your vehicle. A short walk down the shoreline toward the ship channel is one of nature's greatest gifts. Ruddy Turnstones; Least, Royal, and Sandwich Terns; Snowy Plovers; and American Oystercatchers flock together on the small strip of beach to nest, roost, and feed. Because this is a nesting area, the beach is restricted and portions might be closed when certain ground-nesting birds are sitting on their eggs and raising their young. Please take notice of the signs and be respectful to the birds.

American White and Brown Pelicans float on the surf while scaups and scoters rest on the shore in the morning light. Despite being so close to the Houston Ship Channel, the sanctuary is a remarkably peaceful place and can feel remote when you turn your back to the giant tankers. Records indicate that more than three hundred species of birds have been sighted at this location throughout the year. My highest count is eighty-two species in five hours on a calm day in April. It is a beautiful place to take the time to learn the different looks and habits of the shorebirds as they reveal themselves in this protected space. Houston Audubon offers guided walks at this location, so check the website for dates and times.

American Oystercatcher: The defining feature of this black-and-white shorebird is its long, bright orange, blade-like bill. Oystercatchers use the bill to stab into mussels and pry them open. These birds build their nests along the sandy beaches of the Gulf Coast, which makes them susceptible to the hazards of development and increased human activity along the beaches. Courting birds will take romantic walks or jogs along the beach together. Healthy birds can live more than twenty years. They can be found year-round along parts of the Texas coast.

FIGURE 2.11. American Oystercatcher and Willet (photo by Jennifer L. Bristol).

High Island: Boy Scout Woods (339 species)
2088 Fifth Street, High Island, TX 77623
https://houstonaudubon.org/sanctuaries/high-island/boy-scout-woods.html
Parking Lot, Short Trail, Boardwalk, Bird Blind

High Island is famous for "fallouts" during the spring migrations. I have been there twice for a fallout, and it is breathtaking. During my last experience with the Scott Free Family Birds, I declared, "It's raining orioles."

Fallouts occur when our avian friends are flying across the Gulf of Mexico and their tailwind turns into a headwind. A spring norther will cause the birds to drop out of the sky onto the first patch of land they encounter in search of food and fresh water. Under these conditions birds can be exhausted from battling the north wind and light down as quickly as they are able. High Island is just that—a high spot along the barrier islands of the Texas coastline. For centuries, a great stand of oaks has stood as a beacon to the birds to guide them safely to shore.

Birders also flock to this unique natural feature during the migrations. Donned in their drab-colored clothing and wilting under the weight of their gear, the birders mill around the ancient salt dome, hoping to spot a Cape May Warbler or a Warbling Vireo. I frequently tease my husband to ask the "guy in the tan shirt" what he's seeing, which narrows his options down to all but one guy in the group stalking the trees around the Houston Audubon Field Station.

The parking lot at Boy Scout Woods has a mulberry tree that is often filled with tanagers, grosbeaks, and orioles during April and May. Walk down the road a block or so to the Houston Audubon Field Station to purchase your day pass, which allows access to all the High Island birding sites. The yard of the field station is usually filled with vireos and hummingbirds feeding on the blooming bottlebrushes, while American Redstarts and Northern Parulas dance in the tops of the hackberry trees. More than thirty species of warblers pass through the woods of High Island each year during the spring migration. During the same time the less colorful, but equally special Gray-cheeked, Swainson's, Hermit, and Wood Thrushes pass through, searching the ground for insects and worms.

Houston Audubon owns and operates several properties on High Island and has a small visitor center at Boy Scout Woods. Just beyond the gate, there is a pavilion with a bathroom, volunteer station, and bleachers where you can sit and watch birds frequent the drips. Volunteers keep a detailed list of what is being seen in the area on any given day. Houston Audubon offers guided bird walks during the spring, so check its website for times and dates.

Birding at Boy Scout Woods with my mom is always a treat because she knows everyone. Jokingly, we refer to her as our "Celebrity Birder." On our competitive trips we have to schedule an extra hour for her to visit. However, her time spent chatting is always worth it, as her wonderful birding friends happily share their birding adventures and sightings. One of the great things about most birders is their willingness to share information with other birders.

Smith Oaks is just down the road from Boy Scout Woods. The trails are rougher, but there is plenty to see from the parking area. If you are up for a short walk, the rookery is worth a look during April and May when Great Blue Herons, Great Egrets, and Roseate Spoonbills are nesting. There are two good bird blinds where you can sit and watch the action as the birds move about building their nests and raising their young.

Hook Woods Bird Sanctuary off First Street is also a good stop. The small sanctuary has fresh water and large trees that offer birds a good resting point as they arrive from the south.

> ### ⫸ **Feather Fact** ⫷
>
> **Roseate Spoonbill:** This odd pink bird was once hunted almost to extinction, as its wings were popular for making fans for ladies during the Victorian era. The radiant pink color is a result of the bird eating crustaceans that are filled with a particular alga. The bird sweeps its large bill through the water; once prey is found, tiny nerves will detect it and snap the bill shut. The species has made a remarkable comeback but still suffers from loss of habitat. Roseate Spoonbills can be found in all Gulf Coast states.

FIGURE 2.12.
Roseate Spoonbills at the rookery on High Island (photo by Jennifer L. Bristol).

Anahuac National Wildlife Refuge (331 species)
4318 FM 1985, Anahuac, TX 77514
https://www.fws.gov/refuge/Anahuac
Parking Lots, Short Trails, Boardwalk, Bird Blind,
Observation Platform, Driving Tour

For years I have been intimidated by this massive matrix of wetlands and coastal prairies. It always seemed a little too far off the beaten path, and I was never sure what to do when I arrived. It's not the type of terrain to just hike around until you figure out where the birds are. But one evening in April, I found the magic of this immense space.

The Shoveler Pond Auto-Tour Loop is where it's at in Anahuac. Get your binoculars and camera ready to bird right from the car. I like to go just before the start of dusk in the spring to watch the shorebirds and ducks return from the rice fields and nearby wetlands. Dusk is also the time when the light is best for taking good photos of these beautiful creatures. If you decide to get out of your car, don't go far, as there are alligators lurking about.

The driving loop is approximately two miles long and offers a short boardwalk that leads to an overlook about halfway around the pond. The small pond is full of Roseate Spoonbills, White Ibises, Common and Purple Gallinules, Black-necked Stilts, Black-bellied and Fulvous Whistling-Ducks, and Mottled Ducks, along with Red-winged Blackbirds. During the spring migration it is easy to spot orioles, warblers, and hawks passing overhead as well. Because the refuge is on the edge of the great pine forest that stretches north to the Great Plains, it is common to see a Bald Eagle circling over the pond and adjacent fields.

We incorporated this site into one of our birding competitions that included my husband, mother, uncle, and his lady friend. When we arrived at the refuge, we had already been birding close to twelve hours, and needless to say, my team was quickly unraveling. Our first stop along the boardwalk yielded nothing new to our count for the day. My mother suggested we take the short drive as our *last* act of birding for the day. As soon as we crossed the small bridge, we started adding birds to our already long list. My mom had tossed me a Hail Mary pass, and I ran it in for the touchdown.

My uncle's friend, Mary Lee, was so taken with the magic of the pond, the sheer intensity and number of birds, and the glow of the sunset that she still talks about it. The highlight was finally getting to see the elusive and tiny Yellow Rail. It walked right across the road, then disappeared again into the thick reeds. In my enthusiasm, I didn't get a good photo of it, but the memory will last a lifetime.

The refuge was established in 1963 and encompasses thirty-four thousand acres of coastal plains and marshes that provide critical nesting areas for neotropical migrating birds and wintering waterfowl. If ducks are your thing, I recommend visiting the refuge between October and March to see more than twenty-seven species of ducks and geese that winter in the marshes and feed in the agricultural fields to the north. Some reports claim that more than eighty thousand Snow Geese flock to the area in winter and fill the sky in a white cloud. Portions of the refuge are closed to visitors during waterfowl hunting season, so check the website for dates and times.

⫸ **Feather Fact** ⫷

Snow Goose: This large white goose winters in Texas and nests in colonies on the tundra all the way into the Arctic Circle. Snow Geese eat mostly seeds, stems, leaves, grasses, and sedges found in fields and near wetlands. Because they are ground nesters, they are vulnerable to predators and increased human activity; however, their population is strong. Females choose the nesting site, scratch it out on the ground, and can lay an egg within an hour of building the nest.

FIGURE 2.13. Snow Geese filling the sky (photo by Jennifer L. Bristol).

Baytown Nature Center (286 species)
6213 Bayway Drive, Baytown, TX 77520
https://www.baytown.org/city-hall/departments/parks-recreation/baytown-
nature-center
Parking Lots, Nature Center Campus, Short Trails,
Boardwalk, Bird Blinds

This park is a natural gem nestled in the cradle of the "chemical coast," a term affectionately used by Houstonians to describe the ring of oil refineries and chemical plants that rim the coastline. The five hundred–acre nature center has a fascinating history that goes back to the Akokisa Indians who seasonally hunted and fished in the area before the 1830s and the arrival of Europeans.

The park is an example of what happens when humans interfere too much with nature. The area was once a neighborhood of Baytown called Brownwood and was home to about 360 houses, mostly owned by Humble Oil executives and engineers. But mismanagement of water from the bays caused massive subsidence, and hurricanes and storms caused frequent flooding, so the residents were eventually forced to move. The area was declared a superfund site, and wetlands were set aside as mitigation. That is the simplified version of what happened; for more information have a look at *The Texas Landscape Project: Nature and People* by David Todd and Jonathan Ogren.

Today, the small park is home to more than 270 species of birds and other wildlife. This is a good spot to visit pretty much year-round; however, the bugs can get thick during the warmer months. Most of the trails are abandoned roads of the old development, which makes walking easy and flat. I recommend milling around the marshes and butterfly garden at the intersection of Baytown and Crow Roads. Across from the butterfly garden is the Chickadee Trail, which wanders through the dense forest and is filled with migrants during the spring. During the winter it is common to find Yellow-rumped and Pine Warblers, Carolina Chickadees, American Robins, Eastern Bluebirds, Northern Cardinals, White-crowned and Swamp Sparrows, and Cedar Waxwings.

Since the center is surrounded on three sides by bays and has freshwater marshes, there are more shorebirds and gulls than you can shake a stick at. Along the bays it is common to be treated to aerial dances from Black Skimmers or Forster's Terns, while American White Pelicans lumber by in formation. All sizes from the Least Sandpiper to the Sandhill Crane are welcome at this important piece of habitat. There are three good bird blinds in the park where you can set up your camera and snap some amazing photos of the birds and butterflies.

The Children's Nature Discovery Area is a great place to bird-watch while the little ones play; there is even an interpretive sign that shows the wingspans of several of the local birds. As you look out across the bay, you might notice the San Jacinto Monument, where the final battle for Texas independence took place. The San Jacinto Peninsula is also a good place to watch for migrating hawks in the fall as they move through the area along the Mississippi and Central Flyways. If raptors are really your thing, I recommend taking the hour drive around Trinity Bay to the Smith Point Hawk Watch Tower.

I won't lie; it is hard to escape the presence of industrial complexes surrounding the bays. A low humming noise can be heard from all points, and the air has a slight chemical smell and taste. However, it does not detract from the awesome birding.

The center charges an entrance fee, and pets are not allowed inside the park, so plan accordingly. It also offers lots of bird walks, classes, and volunteer opportunities, which are informative and fun. Check the website for current times and dates.

⫸ **Feather Fact** ⫷

Snowy Egret: This elegant, bright white bird was almost lost entirely to the fashion industry of the Victorian era. In the mid-1880s an ounce of its coveted feathers cost more than gold. Thanks to conservation efforts the populations have rebounded, and today Snowy Egrets can be found in shallow wetlands throughout most of Central America and the southern United States. Snowy Egrets have a distinct black bill and legs with large yellow feet, which sets them apart from the larger Great Egret, which sports a yellow bill and legs. It is thought that Snowy Egrets use their large yellow feet to stir up the aquatic life they depend on for food.

FIGURE 2.14. Snowy Egret (photo by Thomas Nilles).

San Jacinto Battleground State Historic Site (302 species)
3523 Independence Parkway South, La Porte, TX 77571
https://tpwd.texas.gov/state-parks/san-jacinto-battleground
Parking Lots, Short Trail, Boardwalk

If you love Texas history and birding as much as I do, then please take the time to visit this location. I can't imagine the conditions that the men of both armies must have suffered through while camping and fighting in the wetlands and coastal prairies during mid-April; it must have been miserable. Oddly enough, the birds would have been in full migration during the final battle of the Texas Revolution. I'd like to think there was at least one soldier who was comforted by the sound of the Eastern Meadowlark or Summer Tanager or delighted by the colors of a Little Blue Heron.

Aside from immersing in the guts and glory of Texas cultural history, the natural history holds an even greater tale. This ecoregion is where the forest, prairie, and wetlands blend together into a mecca for migrating and local birds. It's also a hotspot for bugs, so prepare accordingly if you plan to visit between March and November.

The trail and connecting boardwalk that stretches out into the vastness of the marshes is worth a stroll. There are plenty of places to stop and watch for Great Blue, Green, and Tricolored Herons fishing in the shallow fresh water of the bay. Soras and Clapper Rails can be heard clucking deep in the reeds, while flocks of American Avocets fly in synchronicity on the horizon. The marshes are filled with Least, Western, Solitary, Spotted, Stilt, and White-rumped Sandpipers.

There are plenty of parking areas to explore in this small park. The wooded area where the Mexican army camped is really worth walking around in spring to look for Blue-winged, Blackpoll, Mourning, and Bay-breasted Warblers. While the armies camped in the area during April, more than 190 species of birds could have been found in the very trees that gave the soldiers shade from the Texas sun.

During the winter months Sandhill Cranes, Wood Storks, Greater White-fronted Geese, Buffleheads, and Redheads flock here from the north along with a number of other geese and ducks. The fall is also a good time to watch the skies for Broad-winged, Swainson's, Red-tailed, and White-tailed Hawks or Mississippi Kites and Bald Eagles.

Red-winged Blackbird: This bird is one of the most abundant in North America and can be found wherever wetlands exist. Red-winged Blackbirds are highly social and are polygamous breeders, with a single male having up to fifteen females in his flock. The females are streaky brown birds that look a lot like sparrows, while the males are a rich black with vivid red and yellow bars on their wings. Since publication of Arthur Allen's *The Red-winged Blackbird: A Study in the Ecology of a Cattail Marsh* in 1911, these birds have been the subject of multiple studies about animal communication and social networks.

FIGURE 2.15. Male Red-winged Blackbird (photo by Jennifer L. Bristol).

Sheldon Lake State Park and Environmental Learning Center (283 species)

14140 Garrett Road, Houston, TX 77054
https://tpwd.texas.gov/state-parks/sheldon-lake
Parking Lot, Short Trail, Bird Blind, Observation Platform

Let's talk about ducks. Lake Sheldon State Park and Environmental Learning Center is one of those urban birding jewels hiding in plain sight. It is waterfowl central almost year-round and has plenty of guided walks offered by the knowledgeable volunteers and park staff.

The parking lot is a decent place to bird with plenty of species flying overhead as they pass from the lake to the shallow ponds that remain from an old fish hatchery. There is also a short, flat, half-mile wood-lined trail that loops around the ponds with plenty of places where you can stop and observe. The combination of the lake and the restored prairie makes it a stopping point for ducks, geese, sparrows, and other shorebirds wintering along the coast. Wood Ducks and Pied-billed Grebes can be found year-round, while Mallards, Cinnamon Teals, Canvasbacks, Ring-necked Ducks, and Lesser Scaups, along with more than twenty other species of waterfowl, grace the lakes from November to March.

On a nice day during the fall or spring, take the short walk along the ADA-accessible path to the John Jacob Observation Tower that rises sixty feet above the coastal prairie. It offers an ideal vantage point where you can watch for Red-tailed Hawks and Black and Turkey Vultures. The tower looks out over the lake, old fish hatchery ponds, and restored prairie. Worried about climbing a lot of stairs? Don't be. The tower is equipped with an elevator to make it accessible to everyone. The park is free and open to the public all year.

Red-tailed Hawk: A wise keeper of the hawk watch tower of Bentsen–Rio Grande Valley State Park once told me to assume that any hawk you see is a Red-tailed Hawk until you can prove otherwise. This large raptor is the most common hawk in North America and has adapted well to urban living. If you think you might be seeing the same hawk year after year on the same light pole on your drive to work, you might be. Red-tailed Hawks can live up to thirty years. Their shrill call is used in movies for just about every type of bird from eagles to ravens and always seems to be present when a Native American enters the scene.

FIGURE 2.16. Red-tailed Hawk (photo by Thomas Nilles).

3 • Piney Woods

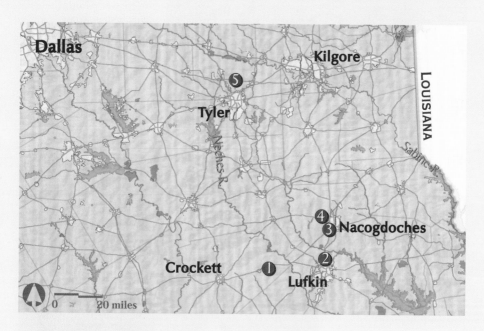

PINEY WOODS REGION
KEY:
1   Ratcliff Lake Recreation Area/Davy Crockett National Forest
2   Ellen Trout Park
3   Pecan Acres Park
4   Pineywoods Native Plant Center and Tucker Woods
5   Tyler State Park

FIGURE 3.1. Male Ruby-throated Hummingbird (photo by Jennifer L. Bristol).

T his region doesn't center around a single major metro as some of the others do; instead, it laces together the agricultural and timber country known as East Texas that is dotted with midsize and small towns. Texas Parks and Wildlife Department defines the Piney Woods region as encompassing twenty-seven counties in the eastern part of the state. What truly defines this ecoregion are the lush pine forests rolling across low hills, mixed with sturdy hardwoods along the bottomlands of the many creeks and rivers. Prior to European settlement, the Caddo and Tejas hunted, gathered, and lived among the towering pines and wide rivers. Earlier settlers cut their way into the forest and slowly changed the region into a mix of farmland and timber plantations.

Glimpses of what the majestic forest might have looked like pre-European settlement can be found in the Davy Crockett, Angelina, and Sabine National Forests or the Big Thicket National Preserve. A monoculture pine forest cannot support a large variety of birds; the forest needs to be mixed with young and old pines, hardwoods, native grasses, and shrubs in order to maintain a thriving bird population. While birding the parking lots, campgrounds, and short nature trails of the region, you might notice that certain native trees or combination of trees and shrubs is more attractive and sustains a greater variety of birds than others. It's worthwhile to note these trees and shrubs because chances are they will be favored by the same or similar birds at other locations you explore.

Ratcliff Lake Recreation Area/Davy Crockett National Forest (124 species)

18551 State Highway 7, Kennard, TX 75847
https://www.recreation.gov/camping/campgrounds/234362 and https://www.fs.usda.gov/detail/texas/about-forest/districts/?cid=fswdev3_008441
Parking Lot, Campground

Let me stress that birding in East Texas is not easy. Nevertheless, Ratcliff Lake has always been a personal favorite nature spot for me. My mother is from East Texas and grew up in Nacogdoches. At least once a year we would travel to the land of tall pines to visit the family homeland. My grandfather loved to picnic at Ratcliff Lake and marvel at the healthy, towering loblolly pines; most of my tree knowledge comes from my grandfather, who was like a walking, talking encyclopedia.

The park pretty much consists of the lake, picnic area, camping loops, and three trails, including the twenty-mile-long 4-C Trail. The Tall Pines and Trail Tamer Trails are shorter but still wander through some pretty dense woods that make birding difficult. I highly recommend limiting your birding to the campgrounds and lake area, as they create open spaces in the dense trees that allow you to actually see the birds.

There are several species of woodpeckers in the forest, but the Pileated and endangered Red-cockaded Woodpeckers are of special interest. The Pileated Woodpecker inspired Warner Brother's "Woody Woodpecker." The birds are easy to spot and hear when they are banging their beaks against the trees while looking for bugs. To me, they look like they just flew in from the Jurassic period. I have never seen the Red-cockaded Woodpecker, but the name is fun to say and the Davy Crockett National Forest is its preferred habitat.

Ratcliff Lake was once the log pond and water source for the Central Coal and Coke Sawmill around the turn of the nineteenth century. The Civilian Conservation Corps built the Ratcliff Lake National Recreation area in 1936; the Davy Crockett National Forest was also dedicated that same year.

The hardwood and pine forest is also home to one of the most entertaining birds ever, the American Woodcock. Please stop reading right now and go to a device where you can access YouTube and look up "Dancing Woodcock." The Woodcock is a treat to see although it is elusive and well camouflaged. Since Woodcocks spend most of their day on the ground, it is best to look for them in winter or early spring before the vegetation gets too thick. Alternatively, you can wait for a slick-looking bird to dance across the parking lot. I laugh every time I see them do their funky little rocking walk.

Pack a lunch and get a good picnic table, or load up the RV or tents and reserve a campsite; either way, the name of the game for birding at this location is "low key." On more than one occasion we saw Wild Turkeys leisurely wander through the picnic area. That is how it happens in the towering pines where patience is a virtue; you have to wait for nature to present itself on its own terms. The same can be said about the people.

≫ Feather Fact ≪

Red-bellied Woodpecker: The name of this medium-sized woodpecker won't help you identify it as it doesn't have a red belly. Instead, it wears a vibrant red cap and has black-and-white wings and back and a plain buff belly. Red-bellied Woodpeckers live exclusively in the United States from Central Texas north to Wisconsin and east to the Atlantic Ocean. Like Acorn Woodpeckers, they store nuts and seeds for winter in trees called pantries. A breeding pair will carve out a new nest in the same tree each year. They have a long, barbed tongue that they trust into crevices and holes in the tree to retrieve insects. They are attracted to feeders that offer the right mix of seeds, nuts, and berries.

FIGURE 3.5. Red-bellied Woodpecker (photo by Jennifer L. Bristol).

Ellen Trout Park (159 species)
402 Zoo Circle, Lufkin, TX 75904
http://cityoflufkin.com/zoo/
Parking Lot, Short Trail

Nestled next to the Ellen Trout Zoo, this small city park encircles a lake that attracts a variety of ducks and geese year-round. The small fields surrounding the lake are good places to find sparrows, Eastern Bluebirds, and American Pipits during the winter months.

The park is fairly open, so it is easy to see the birds gathering at the lake and in the surrounding woods: Canvasbacks, Northern Shovelers, Gadwalls, Green-winged Teals, Ring-necked Ducks, and American Coots are all common in the winter and early spring. Search the shoreline for Great Blue and Green Herons, Great Egrets, and Belted Kingfishers all looking to catch a fish or a frog from the stocked lake. The air above the calm waters fills in the spring and summer with Chimney Swifts, Purple Martins, and Barn and Cliff Swallows, all performing their aerial gymnastics as they feed on insects. If you visit in the winter months, you might catch a glimpse of the pretty little Fox Sparrow that winters in forested areas of Texas and summers in northern Canada and Alaska. This park is a good place to search for the Brown-headed Nuthatch, which can be found only in East Texas and nowhere else in the state. Cornell Lab of Ornithology reports this bird to sound like a rubber ducky and I would agree with that assessment.

Birding around the parking lot is okay, but if you have the time, take a short walk on the crushed-granite trail that circles the lake. There are benches along the way where you can stop and enjoy the birds and the sounds of nature.

Eastern Bluebird: This royal-blue, rust, and buff bird is a delight to see and hear. Eastern Bluebirds typically perch on wires or exposed branches as they wait for an insect to come along so they can swoop down and snatch it up; some birds can see their prey from sixty feet away. In addition to insects, they eat berries and have been recorded eating lizards and frogs as well. These pretty birds can be found year-round across most of Central and East Texas; however, many travel north to the US border states and Canada to breed.

FIGURE 3.6. Male Eastern Bluebird in parking lot of Ellen Trout Park (photo by Jennifer L. Bristol).

Pecan Acres Park (161 species)
826 Starr Avenue, Nacogdoches, TX 75961
https://www.visitnacogdoches.org/listing/pecan-acres-park/251/
Parking Lot, Short Trail

Located on the banks of Lanana Creek, this beautiful twenty-three-acre park is frequented by a surprising number of birds. The Lanana Creek Trail weaves in and out of forest and open spaces that make it easier to see birds in flight, in the trees, and along the ground. The ground is important here because it is where you will find most Hermit Thrushes, Louisiana Waterthrushes, American Robins, Brown Thrashers, and on occasion a Gray Catbird.

During the spring migration the trees fill with hungry warblers heading farther east and north along the Mississippi Flyway: Canada, Tennessee, Nashville, and Kentucky Warblers all dash through the region from April to May alongside Yellow-breasted Chats and Rose-breasted Grosbeaks. Pine and Yellow-rumped Warblers, American Goldfinches, and Chipping and White-throated Sparrows return in late November and stay in the area until mid-May, when they begin their journey north. White-throated Sparrows are easy to spot during the winter months because they stay together in large flocks and feed along the edges of woodlands and fields.

➤ **Feather Fact** ⬅

American Robin: Who doesn't love the song of the Robin? These iconic birds can be found year-round in North Texas or passing through the rest of the state in the spring and fall. They are one of the first birds to arrive in the north and signal the end of winter; however, many choose not to migrate at all and stay in one place all year long. During breeding season they congregate into large roosts. They mostly feed along the ground or on understory shrubs, eating worms, beetles, and berries; in fact, a group of Robins is called a worm.

FIGURE 3.7. American Robin (photo by Thomas Nilles).

Pineywoods Native Plant Center
and Tucker Woods (100 species)
2900 Raguet Street, Nacogdoches, TX 75965
http://sfagardens.sfasu.edu/index.php/pnpc
Parking Lot, Short Trails, Boardwalk

I've spent quite a bit of time at the Pineywoods Native Plant Center and adjacent Ina Brundrett Conservation Education Building for events related to Texas Children in Nature. I never get tired of walking along the boardwalk and paved trails to look for birds and marvel at the towering trees contained in the forty-two-acre garden. The boardwalk crosses a small wetland that attracts Green Herons to the water, while Winter and Carolina Wrens and Song Sparrows flutter about in the tall native grasses. If you visit near dusk in the fall, you might be treated to the who-cooks-for-you call of the Barred Owl.

The best time to bird this small, rich forest is after the leaves start to fall and before they grow thick again in the spring. For me, the best time to visit the area is February, when the air is cool and the winter birds are busy feeding in the bare trees and on the ground. Because the forest is mature and has a good mix of hardwoods and pines, there is an abundance of woodpeckers, sapsuckers, nuthatches, and creepers.

On a side note about the birds of East Texas, I consider the area to be rich with insects. However, there are not as many flycatchers in the region as you might expect. If I were a flycatcher, I would take advantage of the proverbial bug buffet that is East Texas.

Carolina Wren: This chatty little wren can be found over most of Texas with the exception of the far west. The males are constantly vocalizing to the females in courtship and to establish territory while constantly on the move looking for spiders and other insects. To say they are busy little birds is an understatement, as they will build several different nests made of snakeskins, hair, sticks, and feathers to throw off predators. The birds in my yard have luxury nests lined with piles of soft dog hair. A group of these nonmigratory birds is called a chime or flight.

FIGURE 3.8. Carolina Wren (photo by Jennifer L. Bristol).

Tyler State Park (228 species)
789 Park Road 16, Tyler, TX 75706
https://tpwd.texas.gov/state-parks/tyler
Parking Lot, Campgrounds, Short Trail, Bird Blind

Birding in East Texas can be miserable. There, I said it. The thick forest often obscures the birds, and the trees are so tall that it is hard to spot the warblers or other smaller songbirds as they dance through the lofty treetops. By April the bugs are hungry for human blood, and the humidity is oppressive.

However, if you want to see woodpeckers, nuthatches, and owls, you will have to scoot behind the "pine curtain" at some point. Make it easy on yourself and your birding friends by reserving a campsite at Tyler State Park in the spring or fall, deploying a comfortable camp chair, and birding from the campground. The park is busy, but if you have time to camp during the week, it can be a tranquil haven.

I also recommend downloading one of the birding apps on your phone or tablet so you can identify birds from their songs. Better birders than I can bird primarily by song and sound rather than by sight. Personally, I like both but prefer to see and photograph the pretty birds when I can. Remember, never attempt to lure birds by playing the song; that is bad birding behavior.

During the fall and winter the lake draws Buffleheads, Wood Ducks, American White Pelicans, Belted Kingfishers, Ospreys, and a variety of terns and gulls, while the woods are abundant with woodpeckers and sapsuckers year-round. Both migration seasons bring in raptors such as Mississippi Kites; Broad-winged, Red-tailed, and Sharp-shinned Hawks; Ospreys; and Bald Eagles.

If you want a short walk, the Blackjack Nature Trail is a good place for spotting Dark-eyed Juncos, Song Sparrows, and Cedar Waxwings during the winter and Black-throated Green, Pine, Chestnut-sided, and Nashville Warblers during the spring. The Blackjack Nature Trail parking lot, bird blind, and trail are good places to see just about everything the park has to offer. The mix of grasslands and forest allows for a good line of sight to see into the brush and canopy and birds on the wing as they pass overhead. One of the teams competing in the Great Texas Birding Classic reported seeing seventy-seven species of birds at the park in one day.

Barred Owl: This silent flyer can be found across central and eastern parts of North America, with some occurring in the Pacific Northwest. They are best known for their distinctive *who-cooks-for-you* call that can be heard at dusk in the mature forests where they prefer to live. Barreds are a bit of a homebody and will spend the twenty-plus years of their life in a home range of about five to ten miles. Since they are large birds, they need large, mature trees that provide a nest cavity that can accommodate their size. They prefer to eat small game such as mice, rats, squirrels, or other birds; however, they will also fish from time to time if the opportunity presents itself.

FIGURE 3.9. Barred Owl (photo by Thomas Nilles).

4 • Dallas/Fort Worth

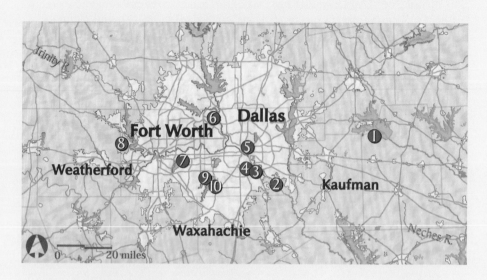

DALLAS/FORT WORTH REGION

KEY:

1   Lake Tawakoni State Park
2   John Bunker Sands Wetland Center
3   Trinity River Audubon Center
4   Dallas: Joppa Preserve/Lemmon Lake
5   White Rock Lake
6   McInnish Sports Complex and Elm Fork Nature Preserve
7   Arlington Village Creek Drying Beds
8   Fort Worth Nature Center and Refuge
9   Cedar Hill State Park
10 Dogwood Canyon Audubon Center

FIGURE 4.1. Vesper Sparrow in the rain (photo by Jennifer L. Bristol).

FIGURE 4.2. Male Painted Bunting (photo by Jennifer L. Bristol).

FIGURE 4.3. Eastern Phoebe (photo by Jennifer L. Bristol).

The North Texas region in this book combines what Texas Parks and Wildlife Department defines as the ecoregions of the Blackland Prairies and the Cross Timbers. However, most of us know the area as the Dallas–Fort Worth Metropolis or just DFW for short.

The land is a mix of prairies, forests, and river bottomlands that were shaped by the mighty Brazos, Trinity, and Sabine Rivers. The Trinity River cuts through both Dallas and Fort Worth and is fed by a myriad of forks and tributaries. People have altered the landscape with their lush lawns, invasive plants, and of course an endless matrix of roads, houses, buildings, agricultural fields, and ranches. Regardless of the centuries of human impact from Native Americans to today, nature persists, and conservation lands, both public and private, help preserve various habitats of prairie, wetlands, cedar breaks, and wooded bottomlands.

Traditionally, the prairie has been a long-undervalued and misunderstood ecosystem. The more I learn about the deep roots of the native grasses, the wildflowers, insects, and wildlife that make up the prairie ecoregion, the more I appreciate them. Far away from the sounds of the city, I still enjoy listening to the wind pass lightly through the grasses of the prairie.

Lake Tawakoni State Park (274 species)
10822 FM 2475, Wills Point, TX 75169
https://tpwd.texas.gov/state-parks/lake-tawakoni
Parking Lots, Campgrounds, Short Trails, Bird Blind

This 376-acre park boasts more than five miles of shoreline along the lake that is formed from the Sabine River. The bottomlands were flooded in the 1960s to create the reservoir, which is now surrounded by a mix of forests and prairie that brings in the birds year-round.

May is really the best time to visit the park for birding. On the Global Big Day on May 5, 2018, one eager birder reported sixty-six species of birds from this location. In addition to the campgrounds and day-use areas, the park has three wildlife-viewing areas off Red Oak, Spring Point, and White Deer Trails. The trails are well maintained, flat, and short in length; however, you prefer to stick to the paved areas, the campgrounds offer a good walking loop that meanders through an assortment of habitat where you can see plenty of birds. The parking lots and day-use areas are all linked by paved trails that offer a solid view of the lake and pass through a grove of trees that always seems busy with birds.

If you do visit the park in April and May, prepare to get warbler neck: Tennessee, Canada, Mourning, Chestnut-sided, Prothonotary, Wilson's, Blackpoll, and Hooded Warblers are easy to locate as they pass through, decked out in the splendor of their breeding colors. The lake also supports a variety of shorebirds such as Least, Spotted, Pectoral, Upland, and White-rumped Sandpipers, along with Lesser Yellowlegs and a number of herons. Spring also brings in some unique flycatchers such as Alder, Least, Willow, and Great Crested Flycatchers.

Winter is a fine time to find Canada, Snow, and Ross's Geese; Red-breasted Mergansers; Pied-billed Grebes; and Wood and Ruddy Ducks. Check the trees for Yellow-bellied Sapsuckers, Red-bellied and Downy Woodpeckers, or White-breasted Nuthatches. The lake is also visited by Common Loons in the winter; although they typically don't issue their haunting calls in the winter, they are always exciting to see. When hunting for fish, they can dive up to two hundred feet underwater by pushing air out from their plumage and lungs. Unlike other birds, they have solid bones, so they can withstand the pressure underwater, but that makes them heavier in flight.

When you visit the park, make sure to take a little time to visit the dam area where more than three hundred species of birds have been reported.

☞ Feather Fact ☜

Ring-necked Duck: This dapper black, gray, and white (brown if female) duck can be found in wetlands across the United States, Canada, and part of Mexico. There is not a dramatic ring on this duck's neck; instead, look for the white ring and black tip on its bill. These ducks migrate from Mexico and the southern states to Canada every year to breed and raise their brood. The trip is approximately two thousand miles each way. Because a duck can live up to twenty years, it flies around forty thousand air miles in a lifetime.

FIGURE 4.4. Male and female Ring-necked Ducks (photo by Jennifer L. Bristol).

John Bunker Sands Wetland Center (268 species)
655 Martin Lane, Seagoville, TX 75159
http://www.wetlandcenter.com
Parking Lot, Nature Center Campus, Boardwalk

This nature center and research site is the product of the conservation-minded John "Bunker" Sands (1948–2003), executive director of the Rosewood Corporation, who claimed the best part of his job was managing the land to be productive for cattle and wildlife. He was particularly interested in managing the wetlands to provide habitat for migrating ducks, geese, shorebirds, and songbirds. The result of his dedication to finding the balance between productive ranching methods and sustainable conservation practices is well presented in the information at the nature center.

I'm always impressed with people who care for the land and use their resources to leave a legacy for future generations. The wetland center is a notable building that takes advantage of the best of green building design that blends well with its surroundings. The back deck is a welcoming space to hang out and bird for as long as you like.

I recommend ambling along the looping boardwalk trails to get a closer look at the wintering flocks of Blue-winged Teals, Northern Shovelers, Snow Geese, Mallards, Northern Pintails, and Lesser Scaups. The wetlands and adjacent agricultural fields are filled with waterfowl and a good variety of shorebirds from November to March. The marshes also attract an interesting mix of blackbirds, including Brewer's and Red-winged Blackbirds, Brown-headed Cowbirds, Common and Great-tailed Grackles, and even a few Rusty Blackbirds. I enjoy watching flocks of blackbirds murmur in mass over the fields in winter.

Two of the big "stars" of the wetland are a pair of Bald Eagles that have returned to the area to nest and raise their young. Other raptors such as Merlins, Cooper's Hawks, Northern Harriers, and Peregrine Falcons also enjoy hunting and fishing the wetlands and fields.

The big trees to the west of the nature center are a good place to find a variety of warblers during the spring migration. Spring and summer months are also good times to see a variety of swallows and flycatchers darting about and feeding on the well-cultivated insect population.

The center has limited hours, so make sure to check the website or call ahead before you visit.

Brown-headed Cowbird: This bird isn't very popular, but it is worth noting. Why isn't it popular? Because Brown-headed Cowbirds are parasites that do not build nests of their own but instead will lay up to a dozen eggs in a season in the nests of more than 220 species of birds. The females leave the young to be raised by the host birds, often to the detriment of the offspring of the host bird. The nests of the Black-capped Vireo are a favored host. Cowbirds were once found only in the grasslands of the Great Plains, but as humans expanded agriculture and lawns, the birds have been able to also increase their range and numbers.

FIGURE 4.5. Brown-headed Cowbirds in November (photo by Jennifer L. Bristol).

Trinity River Audubon Center (223 species)
6500 Great Trinity Forest Way, Dallas, TX 75217
http://trinityriver.audubon.org
Parking Lot, Nature Center Campus, Short Trails,
Boardwalk, Bird Blind

The Trinity River Audubon Center is cool, both inside and out. The nature center building is a work of art, and the trails are masterfully designed to take birders on a journey through a variety of habitats in a fairly small space. The main building was designed by architect Antoine Predock and BRW Architects and leaves the impression that it is from another world. Keep in mind that the entire center sits on an old illegal dumpsite that was transformed back to the native blackland prairie and hardwood bottomlands thanks to the conservation efforts of some dedicated individuals.

The center overlooks one of the shallow ponds on the 130-acre property and has a nice boardwalk and viewing platform from which to watch the shorebirds and ducks. Even more compelling is what is located on the other side of the building in the restored prairie area. The prairie is sparrow and bunting heaven: Field, Fox, Harris's, Lincoln's, Savannah, Song, Swamp, White-crowned, and White-throated Sparrows all thrive on the insects and seeds of the little prairie. It is a great place to watch the sparrows and get to know their habits and songs since it is tricky to tell the small brown birds apart by sight.

If you feel up for a nice flat walk, the paved and crushed-granite trails make loops that total approximately three miles and have plenty of places to stop along the way. The northern parking lot has access to the Trinity River Forest Trail and is a good place to watch for hawks and gulls.

Like most nature centers, Trinity Audubon Center does not allow pets. There are restrooms and an indoor learning space located inside the nature center. The center also offers guided walks, including a Night Hike Owl Prowl that I highly recommend taking if you have the time.

Scissor-tailed Flycatcher: This is the state bird of Oklahoma. We don't often think of birds having an economic value beyond hunting, but these birds eat so many grasshoppers that it is considered a benefit to the agriculture industry. Males perform elaborate sky dances for the females to attract a mate. Their breeding and summer range includes Texas; the range is also in the heart of tornado alley, which makes the birds susceptible to extreme weather. According to the 2014 North American Breeding Bird Survey, the population is decreasing but has not yet been placed on the watch list. A group of scissor-tails is called a zipper.

FIGURE 4.6. Scissor-Tailed Flycatcher on barbed-wire fence (photo by Jennifer L. Bristol).

Dallas: Joppa Preserve/Lemmon Lake (214 species)
Texas Loop 12 Service Road, Dallas, TX 75241
https://www.dallascounty.org/departments/plandev/openspaces/locations/08-joppa.php
Parking Lot, Short Trail

This is about as urban a birding experience as you will get but worth a look. Tucked away on the industrial side of Dallas just off the Great Trinity Forest Way, this small lake is part of a series of lakes and ponds found along the Trinity River. On the day we visited in early November, there were more than one hundred American White Pelicans feeding and bathing in the quiet waters as they pass through on their journey south. The lake is approximately twenty yards from the parking lot and has a paved trail that runs along one side. Admittedly, the parking lot is rough looking. However, the lake is peaceful and has several benches along the paved trail where you can stop and watch the ducks, herons, pelicans, and coots.

When we visited, the thick woods that surround the lake were busy with American Robins, Dark-eyed Juncos, Northern Cardinals, and even a Pileated Woodpecker. Killdeer, Great Blue Herons, and Great Egrets can be found year-round at this park and in the region, while migration can bring additional shorebirds such as Least, Stilt, and Upland Sandpipers; Lesser Yellowlegs; and Semipalmated and American Golden-Plovers. From what I can gather from locals, the birding is best during the summer when Dickcissels, Summer Tanagers, Indigo and Painted Buntings, and Prothonotary Warblers nest in the area.

Like many urban birding locations, this one has plenty of European Starlings and Rock Pigeons loitering about. Both are transplants from Europe, so they do not migrate and seem to thrive in urban centers. Rock Pigeons first arrived in North America in the 1600s with the first Europeans and increased their population with each arriving ship. European Starlings were brought to North America in the 1890s by someone who thought the United States would be improved if only it had birds found in Shakespeare's writings. The Shakespearean groupie released one hundred of the birds in Central Park. Today, it is estimated that there are more than two hundred thousand million of these birds in North and Central America.

If you are into pedal-power birding (birding while biking), this is a great place for that activity. The paved trail along the lake is part of the larger Trinity Forest Trail system.

≫ Feather Fact ≪

American White Pelican: This bird is in decline because of loss of habitat and the use of pesticides. White Pelicans can weigh up to thirty pounds and can hold up to three gallons of water in their long yellow bill. Once they scoop a fish out of the water, they point their bill downward so the water drains out, leaving only the fish, which they toss back into their throat. White Pelicans winter in Texas along the Gulf and in freshwater lakes and summer along the Rocky Mountains from Colorado to Canada. A group of pelicans is called a brief or squadron.

FIGURE 4.7. American White Pelicans (photo by Jennifer L. Bristol).

White Rock Lake (288 species)
2121 Winsted Drive, Dallas, TX 75214
https://www.dallasparks.org/235/White-Rock-Lake
Parking Lots, Short Trails

This is one of Dallas's premier parks and can be crowded on weekends. However, it is worth a visit any time of year. If you have only a short while to bird, I recommend the parking lot off Winsted Drive near the end of the lake where the spillway is located. There are two large viewing platforms on either side of the spillway along White Rock Lake Trail where you can watch the shorebirds and ducks. On the day we visited in the fall, there were hundreds of Ring-billed Gulls hanging out on the spillway with American Coots and Wood Ducks.

This location is also referred to as the Old Fish Hatchery and has 275 species of birds recorded in eBird. Some of the fall/winter birds include Bufflehead, Redhead, Canvasback, Northern Shoveler, Ringed-necked, and Wood Ducks; Eastern and Spotted Towhees; Yellow-bellied Sapsuckers; Cooper's Hawks; and even Bald Eagles.

A historical marker at the viewing platform describes the long and colorful history of the lake, which was created in 1910 as the water source for Dallas after a water shortage occurred. During the 1930s the Civilian Conservation Corps began construction on the lakeshore amenities, and in 1943 the buildings on Winfrey Point were used to house World War II prisoners of war, including those from the Desert Fox's (German general Erwin Rommel) Afrika Corps.

The Big Thicket Grove off Lawther Drive is also a good spot to see American Robins, White-crowned Sparrows, Ruby-crowned Kinglets, and Downy Woodpeckers during the fall and winter months (which in Texas can take place all in one month). During the spring migrations the trees are filled with warblers, vireos, orioles, and flycatchers. This is a true parking lot birding stop. Simply pull up, park, and look up into the massive trees.

The parking lot at Sunset Bay (Pelican Point) is a great place to see herons, ducks, and geese in the fall. The short walk down the pier gives a better vantage point to see the waterfowl and to look back into the trees along the shoreline to see other species.

On my visit I did not have time to walk the grounds of the Dallas Arboretum, although I am told there is decent birding there. Please note that you may have difficulty locating a restroom at any of these stops in the park.

Wood Duck: You will see a number of Wood Duck nesting boxes in parks, wildlife refuges, and nature centers where they are trying to improve the population numbers of this colorful duck that was almost hunted to extinction in the late nineteenth and early twentieth centuries. These vibrant ducks have bounced back thanks to large-scale conservation efforts and enforced hunting regulations. Traditionally the ducks nest in the cavity of trees near a body of fresh water. While some ducks migrate from Texas to other parts of the United States, they can be found year-round from Texas to Florida. Groups of Wood Ducks are called flushes or paddles.

FIGURE 4.8. Male Wood Duck (photo by Jennifer L. Bristol).

McInnish Sports Complex and Elm Fork
Nature Preserve (250 species)
2335 Sandy Lake Road, Carrollton, TX 75006
https://www.cityofcarrollton.com/departments/departments-g-p/parks-recre-
ation/parks-trails-and-natural-areas/elm-fork-nature-preserve
Parking Lots, Short Trails

At first glance this might seem like a giant sports park. Look closer and you will find little pieces of the prairie and wooded bottomlands of the Elm Fork of the Trinity River. In fact, the forty acres of land that form the Elm Fork Nature Preserve were originally purchased as a "woodright" in the 1860s but were never clear-cut. When the land was gifted to the city in 1986, it was described as having its own self-contained ecosystem.

Begin in the parking area near the dog park and walk toward the ponds to observe the fields where the grasses are alive with ground birds fall through spring. The pond yields Canada Geese, Blue-winged Teals, Mallards, and Lesser Scaups from November to April. Resident birds of the wetlands include Great Blue, Little Blue, and Yellow-crowned Night-Herons. The mix of grasslands and forest provides a bounty for flycatchers such as Least, Great Crested, and Scissor-tailed Flycatchers; Eastern and Western Kingbirds; and Northern Mockingbirds that prey on insects from spring to fall. The grasses also support ground feeders such as American Pipits, Dickcissels, Northern Cardinals, Indigo Buntings, and Blue Grosbeaks during the spring and summer. Baltimore Orioles; Summer Tanagers; and Nashville, Bay-breasted, and Yellow Warblers all add a splash of color to the woods along the river and lakes during the spring migration.

At the preserve there is a nature center and bird blind in addition to the looping trails that meander through the woods that offer a peaceful place to escape from the dizzying pace of the DFW metro area.

≫ Feather Fact ≪

Northern Mockingbird: This gray-and-white vocal bird is the state bird of Texas and a few other states, such as Arkansas, Florida, Mississippi, and Tennessee. Mockingbirds are fearless when protecting their territory or nest and can be seen dive-bombing hawks, house pets, snakes, and even a human or two. I always know that spring has officially arrived when I start hearing the males singing away in the middle of the night. Because they are omnivores, they can easily adapt to urban habitats.

FIGURE 4.9. Northern Mockingbird eating prickly pear cactus (photo by Jennifer L. Bristol).

Arlington Village Creek Drying Beds (302 species)
1501 NW Green Oaks Boulevard, Arlington, TX 76012
https://www.greensourcedfw.org/events/dfw-urban-wildlife-village-creek-drying-beds-arlington
Parking Lot, Wastewater Treatment Facility

If you enjoy the smell of drying waste, then this is your place. "Drying Beds" is not a code name for a spa treatment or bowl to dip your feet in to let your nail polish dry after a pedicure. It refers to the place where waste goes to dry and be recycled into who knows what.

The good news is that the drying beds are filled with bugs and shallow pools that attract approximately three hundred or more species throughout the year. Surprisingly, even in the heat of summer it is easy to spot at least thirty species during a quick visit. Late April and early May seem to be the best time to catch the songbird migrants such as Rose-breasted Grosbeaks; Blackburnian, Nashville, and Wilson's Warblers; and American Redstarts. During the winter the drying beds are filled with Winter Wrens, Horned Larks, Snow Geese, Hooded Mergansers, and even passing Sandhill Cranes.

There isn't much space to park, but once you do, haul yourself and your gear twenty-five feet up the small hill and start searching the various basins. If you really can't deal with the smell or arrive after the 4:30 p.m. closing time, scoot next door to River Legacy Park, where you can bird from several parking lots and pavilions. The River Legacy Living Science Center is connected to the park and offers birding walks and other nature classes for adults and children. Check its website for times and dates.

There is no restroom at this location, and pets are not allowed. If you are traveling with your pet, I recommend birding at River Legacy Park instead of the drying beds. The entrance to the drying beds is 0.9 mile south of the River Legacy Park South Entrance.

Horned Lark: The male of this cool little brown bird has feathers on top of its head that look like little horns, and he wears a nefarious black mask across his yellow head. The females instigate and perform the courtship. Horned Larks often forage along grassy areas in pairs, and in the winter months they form larger flocks called a chattering or happiness. They are one of the few birds acclimated to live from sea level to an altitude of thirteen thousand feet. Despite their large range across Mexico, the United States, and Canada, their population is in steep decline, and the reasons for that change are not yet entirely clear.

FIGURE 4.10. Male Horned Lark without visible horn feathers (photo by Jennifer L. Bristol).

Fort Worth Nature Center and Refuge (258 species)

9601 Fossil Ridge Road, Fort Worth, TX 76135
https://www.fwnaturecenter.org/
Parking Lot, Short Trails, Boardwalk, Bird Blind

At the thirty-six hundred–acre Fort Worth Nature Center and Refuge you'll find something almost as cool as birds—the majestic American bison. The center has a small herd of bison to help manage the restored prairie area that covers much of the higher elevations of the park. The staff and volunteers have done an amazing job restoring the grasslands and hardwood bottomlands. The native plants create a healthy environment for birds to gather and raise their young, while also giving visitors a glimpse of what the region would have looked like before it was settled. This land was designated a park around 1915 and contains several Civilian Conservation Corps structures.

The building of the visitor center features several bird feeders and water drips that allow you to easily see a variety of birds from a comfortable space. The center also offers several bird-related educational programs. Occasionally it offers a program about the prairie restoration and what that has done to benefit the migratory and resident birds; I recommend attending if you get a chance.

You don't have to hike the entire twenty miles of trails the park offers to see great birds. Down along the Marsh Boardwalk Trail in the spring it's easy to find Marsh Wrens, Snowy Egrets, American Coots, Soras, and Red-winged Blackbirds. Even in late spring a good variety of ducks will gather in the marshes. There is a second board-walk off Shoreline Drive that spans out over the West Fork of the Trinity River.

During the spring and summer the woods and fields come alive with the songs and calls of White-eyed Vireos, Yellow-billed Cuckoos, Northern Mockingbirds, Painted Buntings, and Summer Tanagers. It's also common to find Hooded, Kentucky, Magnolia, and Yellow Warblers; Yellow-breasted Chats; and Northern Parulas passing through between April and June. Late fall is the best time to wander around the Prairie Trail to look for sparrows or search the skies for passing Snow Geese or Sandhill Cranes.

The center does have limited hours and charges an entrance fee, so be prepared for both. The center has an active friends group that supports the care of the bison herd, birds of prey exhibit, and restoration of historic Civilian Conservation Corps structures. Thanks to my dad for helping raise the funds to support this important piece of history and habitat.

Killdeer: This shorebird prefers the grasslands to the seashore and can be found across Central and North America. Killdeer nest on the ground, and parents will often try to lure away predators with a broken-wing act and a shrill *kill-deer* cry. I've watched a Killdeer charge my horse in an effort to keep her away from the nest; apparently this is a common technique to shoo away large hoofed animals. Killdeer have a distinguishing black-and-white ring around their brow and neck, as well as a rich red eye.

FIGURE 4.11. Killdeer (photo by Jennifer L. Bristol).

Cedar Hill State Park (206 species)
1570 West FM 1382, Cedar Hill, TX 75104
https://tpwd.texas.gov/state-parks/cedar-hill
Parking Lot, Campground, Short Trails

The vegetation and terrain at Cedar Hill State Park are similar to those of Dogwood Canyon Audubon Center with one big exception—the lake. Established in 1989 the 7,740-acre Joe Pool Lake is a favorite recreation reservoir for the greater Dallas–Fort Worth metro. The cedar breaks, limestone hills, and freshwater lake make this a favorite place for birds too.

I've visited the park in both the fall and early spring and have always been pleased with the array of birds. Northern Shovelers, Blue- and Green-winged Teals, American Wigeons, Red-breasted Mergansers, Ruddy Ducks, and a variety of geese all flock to the human-made reservoir.

The grassy fields around the parking lots and day-use areas are a good place to see and hear Fox, Field, Lincoln's, Harris's, and Vesper Sparrows. If you have the time to stroll the campgrounds during the winter and early spring, the trees are alive with Ruby-crowned Kinglets, Cedar Waxwings, Red-eyed Vireos, House Finches, and American Goldfinches. Spring and summer also host a variety of swallows such as Northern Rough-winged, Bank, Cliff, Tree, and Barn Swallows. Each type of swallow feeds on thousands of insects every day. I don't want to even imagine what a hot, humid Texas evening would be like without these insect-eating birds.

This location can get very busy with people in the summer and during warm weekends in the spring and fall. The best time to visit is during the week when the park isn't so hectic. Additionally, the lake is rimmed with several other city and county parks that are worth checking out if you have the time.

➤ Feather Fact ➤

Northern Shoveler: Commonly known as "Shovelers," these ducks winter in Texas and most southern states. They nest from Oklahoma to Alaska during the summer months, where they make a small depression in the ground to lay their eggs. Their large bill is their defining feature, and they can often be seen shoveling in a collective pinwheel formation in an effort to bring food up to the surface of the water. A group of Shovelers is called a flush or raft. They are considered a game bird with a stable population.

FIGURE 4.12. Northern Shovelers napping (photo by Jennifer L. Bristol).

Dogwood Canyon Audubon Center (135 species)
1206 West FM 1382, Cedar Hill, TX 75104
http://dogwood.audubon.org
Parking Lot, Nature Center, Short Trail

This is another property owned and managed by Audubon Texas. Like the Trinity Audubon Center, there are plenty of guided hikes and classes for all ages and abilities to enjoy at the center throughout the year. The center is located in the hills above Joe Pool Lake, which gives it a unique setting.

The cedar breaks are a hangout for spring and fall migratory birds. Some of the year-round common birds include Mourning Doves, Northern Cardinals, Carolina Chickadees, Tufted Titmice, and Downy Woodpeckers. From November to January this is a good spot to look for Red-breasted Nuthatches and Brown Creepers. The center's short walking trails allow visitors to immerse themselves in nature and escape the giant metropolis. The best birding is located close to the nature center and in the tall grasses surrounding the parking area. On a quiet day, the picnic tables at the Nature Play area is a relaxing place to just hang out and enjoy the birds. The Nature Play area is also a cool place to let kids play and explore if you are birding with young ones.

The thick cedar and elm forest can make it difficult to see the birds at first glance. Slow down, walk an easy pace, and stop to listen; the birds will reveal themselves to you. If you are lucky and are looking in the leaves during the winter months, you might be able to spot the elusive American Woodcock.

Painted Bunting: By far one of the most beautiful songbirds, male Painted Buntings are electric-blue, scarlet-red, and vibrant green, while the females are primarily vibrant green with a pale yellow eye ring. Like most buntings, they primarily eat seeds except during breeding season, when they will fuel up on insects. Texas, Oklahoma, and Louisiana are the preferred breeding areas for these colorful birds. They are one of the few songbirds that molts, or sheds its breeding plumage, during the fall migration and not before. Because of their radiant beauty, these birds have a long history of being trapped and sold as cage birds; some still suffer that fate in Central America.

FIGURE 4.13. Male Painted Bunting taking a bath (photo by Jennifer L. Bristol).

5 • Austin and Central Texas

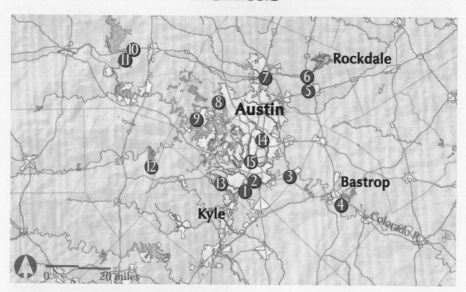

AUSTIN AND CENTRAL TEXAS REGION
KEY:

1   McKinney Falls State Park
2   Hornsby Bend Bird Observatory
3   Webberville Park
4   Bastrop State Park Complex
5   Murphy Park
6   Granger Lake
7   Berry Springs Park and Preserve
8   Devine Lake Park
9   Balcones Canyonlands National Wildlife Refuge
10 Inks Lake State Park
11 Inks Dam National Fish Hatchery
12 Pedernales Falls State Park
13 Lady Bird Johnson Wildflower Center
14 Copperfield Nature Trail
15 Highland Mall ACC Campus and Capital Plaza Parking Lots

FIGURE 5.1. Great Horned Owl chicks at the Lady Bird Johnson Wildflower Center (photo by Jennifer L. Bristol).

FIGURE 5.2. Monk Parakeets (photo by Jennifer L. Bristol).

FIGURE 5.3. Male Green-winged Teal (photo by Jennifer L. Bristol).

FIGURE 5.4. Ruby-crowned Kinglet (photo by Jennifer L. Bristol).

C entral Texas is sometimes referred to as the Hill Country, but for this book it is mostly everything in the orbit of Austin. The ecology of the region is divided down the middle into the Edwards Plateau to the west and the Blackland Prairies and Lost Pines to the east. I live in the transition zone between the Edwards Plateau and the Blackland Prairies and am fascinated by which birds prefer the open spaces of the prairies to the rugged, intimate spaces of the cedar breaks and oak mottes that blanket the hills.

Long before Europeans arrived, Native Americans lived and hunted the region, which supported abundant wildlife and edible native plants. The first European settlers found the craggy limestone hills a challenge to farm and ranch; they preferred the lands to the east that offered rich black soil and river deposits. Even when I was a child growing up in the Austin area, I recall western Travis County being only lightly populated because it was a challenge to build on the steep slopes or blast out a well through the thick limestone. All that has changed as Central Texas continues to be one of the fastest-growing regions in the country.

Humans have changed the land of Central Texas, but the birds still seek native seeds, berries, fruits, insects, small animals, and fresh water that the region has supplied since long before we arrived. Gone are the days when bison herds grazed along grass-lands that skirted the Edwards Plateau. We might not have a chance to see the roaming herds; however, we can still be treated to the migrating birds that spill through the region each spring and fall or choose to call Central Texas home year-round.

McKinney Falls State Park (252 species)

5808 McKinney Falls Parkway, Austin, TX 78744
https://tpwd.texas.gov/state-parks/mckinney-falls
Parking Lot, Campground, Short Trails

This urban state park sits along the banks of Onion Creek and has been frequented by humans for more than five thousand years. The unique limestone features might make it appear to be part of the Edwards Plateau, but it is in fact still in the Blackland Prairies. Just south of the park is an extinct volcano called "Pilot Knob" that helped create the carved limestone shield and rock shelter that are the defining geological features of the park.

The land included in the park and surrounding community was part of a forty-nine thousand–acre land grant purchased from the Mexican government by Santiago del Valle. Since the early 1700s the location has witnessed travelers following El Camino Real de los Tejas, speeding along Highway 71, or embarking from the Austin airport; it seems fitting that it remain a place where people can camp and visit as they have done for centuries.

One of the birding teams I participated with won the Big Sit competition (yes, that's a thing) several years in a row from this location. The Twittering Chats comprised Texas Parks and Wildlife staff, so you can imagine that it was a stellar team. I saw lots of birds but was never fast enough to be the first to call out their name while surrounded by such talented biologists, educators, and resident lawyer-birder Bob. Even without a team of biologists, it is easy to find the birds along the paved and crushed-granite nature trail that meanders along Onion Creek and throughout the park.

Many common species such as American Crows, Roadrunners, Blue Jays, Northern Mockingbirds, Carolina Chickadees, and Northern Cardinals can be found around the parking lots, campground, and trails throughout the year. The Green Kingfisher has moved into the area and can be seen year-round along the creek in addition to Belted Kingfishers, Great Blue Herons, and Double-crested Cormorants. Purple Martins and Barn and Cliff Swallows sweep the skies for insects, while Eastern Phoebes and Western Kingbirds leap from their perches to feed along the emerald-green creek from April to October.

December brings in a combination of three of my favorite birds: Cedar Waxwings, Ruby-crowned Kinglets, and American Goldfinches. I call the Cedar Waxwings the "cool kids" because it looks like they are wearing sunglasses and they are always hanging out in a little gang. All three birds can be seen busily working the trees and shrubs for seeds and insects down along the creek or around the campground.

Mourning Dove: I affectionately call one of the Mourning Doves that lives in my yard "Pink Foot" because of his bright pink legs and feet, a characteristic of the bird. These slender, gray birds with black spots on their back can be found all across North American and most of Central America. Many of the birds in Texas are year-round residents; however, northern birds do migrate south during the winter. Because of their wide distribution, they are also the most hunted dove across the Americas. As they feed on seeds along the ground, they store them in the crop in their neck until they are ready to digest them. Look on telephone wires or fences for them perched in groups of three or more. These hardy birds can live up to thirty years.

FIGURE 5.5.
Mourning Dove with full crop (photo by Jennifer L. Bristol).

FIGURE 5.6.
Mourning Doves at dusk (photo by Jennifer L. Bristol).

Hornsby Bend Bird Observatory (343 species)
2210 South FM 973, Austin, TX 78725
https://www.hornsbybend.org
Parking Lot, Wastewater Treatment Facility, Short Trail,
Bird Blind, Driving Tour

This is a birder's paradise. The intense smell of the waste-settling ponds keeps all other outdoor enthusiasts at bay, so the birds and the birders have it all to themselves. By all accounts, this is a birding hotspot. The shallow ponds are surrounded by fields that drop off to the forested bottomlands along the Colorado River; between the ponds and the river are some of the most spectacular specimens of the Texas State Tree—the pecan.

Not everything that flies past this spot is a bird. The busy Austin airport is located south of the facility, and jets of all sizes fly over day and night as more than a million people a month pass through. Even though it seems to be an industrial wasteland, it is easy to walk a few yards into the embrace of the pecan groves and feel calmed by nature.

Located just east of Austin along the big bend in the Colorado River, this stop is good year-round, but please save your nose and do not visit during July or August, as the smell from the waste ponds can be intense in the sweltering summer heat.

Early in our birding foray, my husband and I traveled to the site. We were excited to see every bird even though we could name only about ten. A woman drove up next to us and inquired if we had seen much. My husband bubbled over with enthusiasm to tell her the few birds we could report and then asked about a bird that darted by.

"Oh. Those are just the yellow rumps," she said, as she pulled her heavy hand-knit cap tighter over her thick gray hair. "Have you seen the Vermilion Flycatcher?" she asked dryly.

"No! Where did you see that?" Thomas eagerly answered.

"Oh, you know. It's down in the usual place," she said as she pulled away. Clearly, she had sized us up as novice birders and was in a hurry to get away from the likes of us. Despite her demeanor, she did help us correctly identify the Yellow-rumped Warbler and put us on to the striking Vermilion Flycatcher.

But you don't even have to get out of your car to see a myriad of species. You can just drive along the banks of the wastewater ponds and see shorebirds, swallows, ducks, and flycatchers. If you want to see the warblers and sparrows, you will have to get out of your car.

What might surprise you the most about this location is the number of shorebirds that frequent the ponds during migration or year-round. From March to October Baird's, Least, Pectoral, Semipalmated, and Western Sandpipers; American Golden-Plovers; Black-necked Stilts; and American Avocets all feed from the shallow ponds. The ponds and river also support more than twenty species of waterfowl.

Along the ponds closest to the river there is a bird blind with benches that offers a shaded spot to look for species. Across from the blind is a Chimney Swift tower and a short trail that leads down into the pecan groves and to the Colorado River. The trail makes several loops in and out of the pecan bottom and connects back with the road that circles the ponds. During the spring migration I have spotted Yellow, Nashville, and Black-and-white Warblers; Blue Grosbeaks; and Painted Buntings along the path and in the grand trees. During the fall and spring migrations keep your eyes on the skies for passing flocks of American White Pelicans, Ring-billed Gulls, and Sandhill Cranes.

The parking lot of the office building is also a great birding spot, as the Purple Martin houses are always busy in spring and summer. Scattered around the yard are several blue birdhouses that often have the lovely little birds perched on top of them during the fall and winter months. The fields that stretch out from the parking lot often have Red-shouldered and Red-tailed Hawks or Crested Caracaras circling overhead, while Chipping, Field, and Savannah Sparrows dance in and out of the grass.

Travis Audubon has frequent field trips to this location, which I recommend checking out.

≫ Feather Fact ≪

Yellow-rumped Warbler: There are two forms of Yellow-rumped Warbler: Myrtle (East) and Audubon's (West). These warblers are common in most parts of North America and can digest 80 percent of all wax-coated berries. They are considered to be the most versatile foragers of all warblers and will eat insects, berries, or seeds. They are also capable of wintering farther north than any other warbler. During the winter they form large flocks called a bouquet or confusion. Because their colors can change greatly throughout the stages of their life, it is easy to mistake them for other warblers; however, their defining feature is the bright yellow spot on their rump.

FIGURE 5.7. Yellow-rumped Warbler in non-breeding colors (photo by Jennifer L. Bristol).

Webberville Park (263 species)
2305 Park Lane, Webberville, TX 78621
https://parks.traviscountytx.gov/parks/webberville
Parking Lot

When I think of this park, I think of one word: mowed. The park is in a lovely pecan bottom along the Colorado River, but the park staff do so love to mow it. I recommend parking at the end of the parking area closest to the river and strolling around.

The park is also known for a good variety of woodpeckers, including the sizable Pileated Woodpecker. During the spring and fall, the huge trees also attract a variety of warblers and vireos. Because the trees are so large, it can be difficult to spot the smaller birds dancing in the treetops at warbler speed. During the spring it is common to hear the call of White-eyed Vireos, Painted Buntings, and Eastern Meadowlarks throughout the park, while winter brings in Yellow-bellied Sapsuckers, Northern Flickers, House Wrens, and Eastern Bluebirds. The fall and winter are also a good time to search the fields and skies for all sorts of birds of prey, including Mississippi Kites, Crested Caracaras, and Ospreys.

The Colorado River can also attract waterfowl such as Wood Ducks, American Wigeons, and Green-winged Teals; and I've had good luck spotting Belted Kingfishers, Great Blue Herons, and an assortment of flycatchers by the river. But the main attraction is the pair of Bald Eagles that have built their nest in the area and have returned for several years. And why not? The large trees offer a sturdy platform to build a nest, while the nearby river provides a well-stocked grocery store.

Bald Eagle: In 1782 the newly formed United States designated this powerful raptor as the national bird. By the 1960s there were only around four hundred nesting pairs left in the lower forty-eight states as a result of the chemical DDT and hunting. Today, Bald Eagles have made a comeback and even nest in Texas along rivers and lakes where fish are abundant. In 2007 they were delisted from US Fish and Wildlife's endangered species list. When hunting, they can reach speeds of up to two hundred miles per hour when on a power dive toward prey. Their nest can be up to six feet in diameter and weight up to a ton. Both parents raise the young, and healthy adults can live up to forty years in the wild.

FIGURE 5.8. Bald Eagle (photo by Jennifer L. Bristol).

Bastrop State Park Complex (227 species)
100 Park Road 1A, Bastrop, TX 78602
https://tpwd.texas.gov/state-parks/bastrop
Parking Lot, Campground, Short Trails

As a former resource manager/park ranger for the complex, I have a deep love and appreciation for Bastrop and Buescher State Parks. I changed jobs just three months before the devastating fire of 2011; however, I remained connected with the park as president of Friends of the Lost Pines State Park and dug in to help raise money and volunteers to assist with the recovery efforts for my beloved park. The forest will continue to grow and change, and with it, the wildlife and birds will continue to change as well.

Part of my charge at the park was to manage the eighty-year-old swimming pool and team of teenage lifeguards; I could write an entire book about those follies. I spent four long, hot summers caring for the football-field-sized pool and campus, and it didn't take long to get to know six fine feathered friends who came to visit every day at 6:45 p.m. Six American Crows would show up on cue when the lifeguards blew the final whistle to clear the pool for the evening. The crows helped clean the tidbits of food left by the hundreds of visitors who enjoyed the pool each day. During the off-season they moved to the campgrounds to scavenge; however, they always came to visit me if I was milling around the swimming pool.

The droughts prior to the devastating fires of 2011 (Bastrop) and 2015 (Buescher) killed many of the oldest and largest loblolly pines and hardwood trees, but the fires wiped out hundreds of thousands more. The fires at Bastrop State Park damaged 96 percent of the park's six thousand–plus acres. However, after the fires, the birds returned in droves to feed off the seeds and berries produced by the new growth. For a while there seemed to be a woodpecker on every dead tree, and there were a lot of dead trees.

I've hiked every trail and firebreak in the park and have had my share of blisters along the way. I can assure you that the best birding at both locations takes place around the campgrounds, lakes, overlooks, and historic cabins or off Park Road along Alum Creek. I recommend camping at the Cozy Circle Loop at Buescher State Park during the spring and birding along the road down to the lake.

On one visit our birding team spotted more than sixty species on one day in the complex; most were right at the campgrounds at Buescher State Park. On that same trip, I learned that the Northern Parula and Painted Bunting nest in the area, a fact that eluded me during the years I worked there. I never get tired of sitting around the campfire listening to the rhythmic song of the nocturnally active Chuck-will's-widow, which can be found in both parks from April to August.

I also recommend renting one of the historic cabins at Bastrop State Park. (I'm told

Cabin #3 is haunted but cannot confirm that legend.) It's not easy to get into one of the cabins, as they book up quickly, but it is worth the effort to stay in one of these historic gems.

Recently, the Red-headed Woodpecker has returned and taken up residence along Alum Creek Road and Park Road 1C. The calming waters of Alum Creek are frequented by a variety of birds year-round. There isn't a parking lot here, so be careful when parking your car on the side of the road.

The Pileated Woodpecker is also a resident of both parks and can be heard hammering away on trees, searching for insects, or issuing a loud raspy call that makes it sound more like a pterodactyl than a bird. Yellow-bellied Sapsuckers, Dark-eyed Juncos, Field Sparrows, Spotted Towhees, and Eastern Bluebirds can been seen in the fall through early spring along with Pine Warblers and some very vocal Carolina Chickadees.

Winter is one of the best times to bird the Lost Pines because it is easier to see through the thick underbrush of the forest. The fire brought a return of the grasses that support more insects and produce seeds, which has brought in more species of sparrows, both types of meadowlarks, and more raptors. Even though the lake at Bastrop State Park is gone, there are plenty of ducks, geese, and cranes that pass over the park during the migrations. There are also reports of a pair of Bald Eagles that have moved into the area.

While bigger birds such as crows, hawks, woodpeckers, cranes, and ducks are all fun to see, it is the sound of the Pine Warbler that I associate the most with Lost Pines. The light airy song, mixed with the soft whisper of the pines, is truly a unique nature experience for Central Texas.

> ### ≫ Feather Fact ≪
>
> **Northern Parula:** This small slate-blue, yellow, and buff warbler can be hard to identify as it dances through the top of the tree canopy. Northern Parulas prefer forests where long, wispy moss such as Spanish moss exists, as that is their preferred nesting material. Spiders are their favorite meal, but they will also feast on a variety of other insects. They winter in the Caribbean and along the Gulf of Mexico in Central America and breed in eastern Canada and the United States, including East Texas and the Lost Pines of Bastrop.

FIGURE 5.9. Male Northern Parula in April (photo by Jennifer L. Bristol).

Murphy Park (121 species)
1600 Veterans Avenue, Taylor, TX 76574
https://www.ci.taylor.tx.us/243/Murphy-Park
Parking Lots, Short Trail

Taylor's oldest park was established in the 1880s around the spring-fed creek. The 120-acre park's focal point is City Lake, which is home to plenty of the town's school mascot: ducks. The center of the lake has a small island that is a rookery for herons during the spring and a hangout for domestic geese and ducks the rest of the year.

Plan to park near the lake in the circular parking lot and search the shrubs for sparrows and Northern Mockingbirds, or walk to the lake to see the ducks, geese, and shorebirds. The large trees surrounding the lake attract some migrants during the spring; however, this is blackland prairie and not a big warbler hangout.

From June to September, the park's largest avian population consists of Chimney Swifts that live in the old tower on the south end of the lake. Hundreds of swifts dance like perfectly paired ice-skaters as they regroup in the evening before diving into the old industrial chimney. Thanks to Georgean and Paul Kyle at the Chaetura Canyon Sanctuary for all the work to raise awareness and study the Chimney Swifts in Central Texas. Early August to September is the best time to see them do their aerial dance. In October, it is common for hundreds of American White Pelicans to stop by for a few days.

There are ADA-accessible trails throughout the park, which makes it easy to stroll and bird at a leisurely pace. The paved trail runs several miles throughout the city and connects a number of its parks.

On a side note, my brother filmed a movie here in the 1990s, and I had a cameo in the film as the girl walking her dogs through the park. I was also the art director on his film and a number of others in my early twenties. The movie, *Monster Hunter*, is not about birding, although at one point the lead character, played by David Carradine, claims to be an ornithologist but is actually just psycho.

Chimney Swift: This bird feeds on insects while entirely on the wing. Chimney Swifts nest in chimneys and old smokestacks, and thus there is a movement to keep chimneys open so these insect eaters have places to nest. When in flight they do not appear to have tail feathers and are often described as flying cigars. In the evening they will partner up and glide along together like a graceful pair of figure skaters before they slip into the cavity of a chimney. They winter in the tropics and spend their summers in the central and eastern parts of the United States.

FIGURE 5.10. Chimney Swift nestlings with adult (photo courtesy of Paul and Georgean Kyle; used with permission).

Granger Lake (319 species)
2880 County Road 348, Granger, TX 76530
http://www.swf-wc.usace.army.mil/granger/
Parking Lots, Campgrounds

With more than three hundred species of birds spotted at the many locations this Soil Conservation Service lake offers, I think that I should have a higher bird count than I do. My husband and I have camped several times at Wilson H. Fox campground in early spring, and I would recommend it as a good camping and birding location.

I always seem to be a day late and a dollar short on my visits to the lake. However, the Travis Audubon and Christmas Bird Counts have recorded incredible numbers of birds here. Because this lake has so many places to bird, I recommend reserving a campsite either at Wilson H. Fox campground or Friendship Park and making a day or two out of it. I also recommend going in the late afternoon to early evening during the warmer months to avoid the heat, as the area is blackland prairie and not well shaded.

Willis Creek Park is situated where Willis Creek flows into the San Gabriel River to make Granger Lake. This is also the area where you are most likely to see the majestic, and very endangered, Whooping Cranes in December or March as they migrate through the area. With only a few hundred of the birds left in the world, it is exciting to see them wading through the shallows of the lake or on the wing coming in for a graceful landing. Bonaparte's, Franklin's, and Ring-billed Gulls; Forster's Terns; and American White Pelicans also spend time at the lake during winter months.

The parking lot at the Pecan Grove Wildlife Management Area is a good place to bird from in the area. This is the backside of the Granger Lake Dam where the San Gabriel River spills out from the dam to cut through the blackland prairie.

Red-tailed and Swainson's Hawks, Northern Harriers, American Kestrels, and Ospreys can often be seen from here as they hunt the grasslands or search for fish. Sparrows and warblers are also plentiful, but what is surprising is how many shorebirds there are along the banks of the river in the grasses: Virginia Rails, Soras, Wilson's Snipes, Greater Yellowlegs, and Least Sandpipers all frequent the area in winter.

At Friendship Park you can see many of the same birds as at other locations around the lake, but the advantage of this stop is that the cove provides cover from the winds, which makes it a shelter for ducks and shorebirds. It is a reliable place to look for Hooded Mergansers, Canvasbacks, Buffleheads, Redheads, and Pied-billed and Eared Grebes from November to March.

During April and May the warblers pass through but not in as great numbers as in other locations throughout Central Texas. The flycatchers and shorebirds are more abundant here during migration.

There is one more stop that is worth a mention. The Granger Lake Sore Finger

Wildlife Unit (who knows where that name came from!) is a primitive area that has a parking lot and a roughly mowed path that leads to the lake's edge, but it is not easy walking and there isn't a deck or platform. If you are up for the walk, I recommend it, but make sure you take some water and your cell phone, as it is remote. If you venture out, you will no doubt experience an abundance of birds from November to March.

> ⫸ **Feather Fact** ⫷
>
> **Osprey:** After the US ban of the use of the pesticide DDT in the 1960s, Osprey populations started to recover. They are one of the few North American raptors whose populations are actually rising instead of declining. Look for them in East, Central, and South Texas during the winter around lakes or bays. During the summer they migrate north to build their nests in tall trees, on telephone poles, or on human-made platforms near lakes where they can easily feed on fish. A small group can be found year-round in East Texas. According to the Cornell Lab of Ornithology, one female Osprey was recorded to fly twenty-seven hundred miles in thirteen days from Massachusetts across the Caribbean to French Guiana in South America.

FIGURE 5.11. Osprey (photo by Jennifer L. Bristol).

Berry Springs Park and Preserve (244 species)
1801 County Road 152, Georgetown, TX 78626
https://www.wilco.org/Departments/Parks-Recreation/County-Parks/Berry-Springs-Park
Parking Lots, Campground, Short Trails

There is a lot to like about this three hundred–acre park set around the crystal-clear spring and lined with more than one thousand pecan trees. This Georgetown city park opened in 2005, with the support of Texas Parks and Wildlife Department and a number of other conservation and recreation groups. It is meticulously maintained, which makes it a pleasant place to visit in every season.

There is a surprising variety of habitat in this relatively small space. The main parking lot is on top of the small hill, and next to the lot is a ring of native plants that surround John Berry's grave. During the fall and winter Vesper, White-crowned, and Harris's Sparrows dart in and out of the native shrubs alongside Carolina Wrens. There is also a well-maintained restroom and water fountain near the parking lot.

John Berry was the original Anglo settler who claimed the land and made it his home in 1845. There are several historical markers throughout the park that describe the story of the Berry family and of the first people there: the Tonkawa and Apache. The Native Americans followed a system of springs along the Edward's Plateau as they tracked the bison herds. I can imagine them setting up camp near the springs, feeding on the native pecans and walnuts, catching fish, and telling stories to their children.

The springs create fish-filled, clear pools that bring in Pied-billed Grebes, Great Blue and Yellow-crowned Night-Herons, Snowy Egrets, and Belted Kingfishers along with other fish eaters. Near the springs is a prairie that the Texas Native Plant Society helped restore and maintain. The native grasses and plants attract sparrows and finches year-round with the most abundance occurring in the winter.

The real magic happens in this park during April and May when the neotropical songbirds arrive en masse. The towering pecan trees and fresh water offer an important refueling stop for the migrants: Yellow-breasted Chats, Scarlet and Summer Tanagers, Yellow-billed Cuckoos, Vermilion Flycatchers, and more than twenty types of warbler all make an appearance in the spring. There is even a report of a Great Kiskadee that hangs out in the trees along the creek year-round. There have also been reports of more than twelve species of flycatchers that frequent the area, including the Eastern Wood-Pewee and Olive-sided Flycatcher. American Robins and Eastern and Spotted Towhees also enjoy feeding in the rich leaf litter along the creek edges during the fall.

Much of this information comes from my mother and her friends. When I called to tell her about the park, she said, "Oh, my friend helped them restore the prairie there.

I've been there many times." Silly me thought she might not have heard about the little park. It's hard to move outside the orbit of the Celebrity Birder.

The entire 2.5 miles of trails are ADA accessible and make several small loops that connect the variety of habitat. I only had an hour to spare when I first visited the park in December and was able to see twenty-three species during that time. On a return visit in May I spotted thirty-eight species, including more than a dozen Yellow Warblers feeding in the pecan trees.

≫ **Feather Fact** ≪

Great Blue Heron: A group of herons is called a battery, hedge, or rookery. When they pair up and start building their nest in a cluster of trees or on a safe island in a body of water, the male brings each stick and presents it to the female. She either takes the stick and carefully weaves it into her nest or tosses it out and sends him packing to find another stick. Building the perfect nest can take days. These are the largest herons in North America and can be found year-round in pretty much all parts of Texas that have water. They have been known to hunt for fish in people's koi ponds.

FIGURE 5.12. Great Blue Heron (photo by Jennifer L. Bristol).

FIGURE 5.13. Male Great Blue Heron carrying a stick for the nest (photo by Jennifer L. Bristol).

Devine Lake Park (264 species)
1807 Waterfall Avenue, Leander, TX 78641
https://www.leandertx.gov/parksrec/page/devine-lake-park
Parking Lot, Short Trail

This small forty-five-acre park packs a lot of punch all year and has a good variety of habitat both within the boundaries of the park and stretching out beyond it to the north and west. The urban sprawl of Leander is slowly closing in around the park and Soil Conservation Service lake, but for now it remains a solid birding spot.

There is a short walking trail that makes a loop and is less than a mile long. It is paved for about half of the journey and then is a mulched path for the remaining section. Leading away from the parking lot, the trail first meanders through a stand of large live oak trees down to the edge of the lake. It is worth wandering slowly through the oaks to look for Blackburnian, Black-throated Green, Chestnut-sided, and Magnolia Warblers during April and May.

In July, a surprising number of shorebirds frequent the lake and can be effortlessly spotted from the benches positioned along the shore. Pectoral, Solitary, and Semi-palmated Sandpipers can be found bobbing along the mudflats of the cove while Bank and Barn Swallows blast through the air inches above the water. The summer can be a hot time to bird this area; after all, it is Central Texas. However, the trail weaves along through the forest after leaving the lakeside and can be refreshingly cool in the mornings and at dusk.

During August and September, several uncommon birds for the area pass through the park, such as Say's Phoebes, Black Terns, and Yellow-headed Blackbirds. In addition to seeing common birds like Purple Martins, Chimney Swifts, Common Nighthawks, and Scissor-tailed Flycatchers, you might be treated to an encounter with tanagers, orioles, or a confusion of warblers. The warblers are harder to define in their fall migration when they are in their nonbreeding colors, but some of them, such as the Black-and-white Warbler and Common Yellowthroat, are still easy to identify.

November through February sees a steady parade of ducks, geese, and shorebirds: American Wigeon, Buffleheads, Blue-winged and Green-winged Teals, Canvasbacks, Gadwalls, and Northern Pintails all shuffle through or even spend the winter on the lake. On occasion, Snow and Canada Geese stop over on their journey farther south.

A portion of the trail wanders into the woods and travels along a small stream. The woods and tall grasses along the stream are active with a variety of birds year-round. On one visit on January 1, I was treated to more than a dozen species on this leg of the short walk. Northern Cardinals and American Robins picked through the leaves while

Carolina Chickadees, Tufted Titmice, Golden-crowned Kinglets, Cedar Waxwings, and Blue Jays darted through the brush. While I watched the smaller birds, I noticed that the Blue Jays and American Crows started to mob something. After a good hard look, I could see a Red-shouldered Hawk sitting on a dead tree, fluffed up in her winter feathers and carefully watching the field for a warm meal.

≫ **Feather Fact** ≪

Red-shouldered Hawk: The Red-shouldered Hawk, one of my favorite raptors, is quite talkative and in constant communication with its mate and brood. When chicks hatch, they can poop over the edge of the nest after just five days. They can be found in parts of North America where tall trees and water exist. When they are soaring overhead, look for the rich rusty shoulders and banded tail, or look for them to perch upright on trees, posts, or power lines. They can live more than twenty years in the wild and will return to the same nesting area year after year. Many will migrate to breeding areas in the northeastern states; however, they also nest and live year-round in Texas and across the southeast.

FIGURE 5.14. Red-shouldered Hawk on Christmas Eve (photo by Jennifer L. Bristol).

Balcones Canyonlands National Wildlife Refuge (217 species)
24518 FM 1431, Marble Falls, TX 78654
https://www.fws.gov/refuge/balcones_canyonlands
Parking Lots, Short Trails, Bird Blind

The Balcones Canyonlands National Wildlife Refuge (BCNWR), like all wildlife refuges, is a great example of the importance of conserving large tracts of land to preserve the health and variety of species. Audubon has recognized it as an Important Bird Area. The BCNWR is a patchwork of approximately twenty-seven thousand acres of rugged Hill Country with old-growth Ashe juniper and oak forests, combined with savannas, escarpments, and clear running springs.

The refuge was established primarily to conserve the nesting habitat of two endangered species, the Golden-cheeked Warbler and Black-capped Vireo. However, according to US Fish and Wildlife, at least one-third of Texas' threatened and endangered species live or move through this part of the Hill Country.

The refuge and other Travis County parks, City of Austin Wildland Conservation and Water Quality Protection Lands, and privately owned conservation lands are the engines that support the majority of bird activity in Travis, Burnet, and Williamson Counties. The canyons that fall away from the limestone hills to the Colorado River and adjoining creeks are considered critical habitat for hundreds of species of native plants, insects, birds, fish, and other wildlife.

The refuge is divided into several units. I recommend taking the time to visit each unit, as the habitat varies and supports different resident and migratory birds. The first stop should be the BCNWR headquarters, where the birding is good all year (avoid August; it is too hot.) The parking lot looks out on fields where sparrows, flycatchers, and hawks feed. You can also stroll along the ADA-accessible path toward the creek, which flows into a basin where waterfowl gather in the winter.

Around the corner from the headquarters is Warbler Vista and the Sunset Deck. This spot offers a true example of how the Hill Country around Austin used to look before urban sprawl occurred. The trails are enchanting, yet rugged, and it is hard to see the birds from the trails. I have seen and heard a Golden-cheeked Warbler from the parking lot of the Cactus Rock Trail during early April; the name of the trail should be a clue about what you might see along the way.

The Sunset Deck at Warbler Vista offers a pleasant view of Lake Travis and is positioned so birders can look down into the open woodlands to see Yellow Warblers, Blue Jays, Northern Cardinals, Canyon Wrens, and Great Crested Flycatchers flittering about the treetops.

Doe Skin Ranch is located in another unit at 10645 FM 1174, Bertram, TX 78605. There is a remote and peaceful feeling about this place. From the parking lot there are four short trails; each offers a window into the ranching life that once occurred on the property. The grasslands, spring-fed creek, pond, and cedar breaks all support a variety of birds. Chipping, Savannah, and White-crowned Sparrows, along with Eastern Phoebes and assorted flycatchers, fill the grasslands, while herons and ducks frequent the pond. During the spring migrations warblers and tanagers are abundant and can often be seen at the bird blind along with Painted Buntings. The grasslands can also reveal species such as the American Woodcock, Wild Turkey, Chuck-will's-widow, or Common Nighthawk. During the fall it is easy to spot geese, cranes, and other large birds soar by as they migrate south.

A few notes about the refuge: It offers two amazing birding events hosted by Friends of BCNWR. Sparrowfest takes place in February and offers classes on how to identify the small brown birds. Approximately twenty species of sparrows are identified during the festival. Balcones Songbird Festival takes place in April and offers classes, field trips, and a space to network with fellow birders.

During the year the refuge closes certain units for hunting, prescribed burns, and other wildlife or habitat management purposes, so be sure to check the website for updates. Also, if you suffer from allergies, I would avoid the refuge during late December and early January when the irritating Ashe juniper explodes its wicked pollen into the air.

The refuge is often mistaken as part of the Balcones Canyonlands Conservation Plan, which cobbles together lands from Travis County, City of Austin, Travis Audubon, and the Nature Conservancy to further protect endangered species in one of the fastest-growing urban areas in the country.

I am proud to say that my mother, Valarie Bristol, assisted in creating the Balcones Canyonlands Conservation Plan when she was county commissioner in the 1990s. The ideas she championed and collaborated on were so successful that it became a national model of how to set up endangered species conservation lands that limited negative impact on business and growth. Later, she helped add conservation lands when she worked for Trust for Public Lands and the Nature Conservancy. Her conservation effort spread across Texas and has resulted in thousands of acres of land being set aside for the protection of wildlife, water, and habitats and for the enjoyment of people.

Golden-cheeked Warbler: This is the only migratory bird species with a breeding range exclusive to Central Texas, which means every Golden-cheeked is a native hatched Texan. It is also one of the most at-risk warblers in North America. It prefers the beautiful rolling hills of the Edwards Plateau, to which hundreds of people move every day. From the 1950s to 1970s more than 50 percent of the bird's habitat was turned into agricultural lands, urbanized, or flooded to make the reservoirs and lakes in Central Texas. The warblers require the shaggy bark of mature (forty years or older) Ashe juniper trees to use for building their nests. The warbler feasts on beetles, deer flies, and other insects, which make it an important piece of the food web of the ecoregions it inhabits.

FIGURE 5.15. Male Golden-cheeked Warbler with grasshopper (photo by Jennifer L. Bristol).

Inks Lake State Park (210 species)
3630 Park Road 4 West, Burnet, TX 78611
https://tpwd.texas.gov/state-parks/inks-lake
Parking Lot, Campgrounds, Short Trail, Bird Blind

I really like this park. It's hard to get a campsite when the weather is nice but worth the effort. The birding here has always been good, but the addition of a state-of-the-art bird blind on the northern side of the lake takes it up a notch. The blind was funded by the local Texas Master Naturalist Chapter and other park volunteers who support the needs of the park that cannot be met by limited state budgets.

The new bird blind has its own gated parking area. You will need to get the code from the ranger at the front office when you check in. Once you park in the small lot, there is a short, unpaved walk to the blind. I recommend spending at least an hour to see what comes to the feeding and watering stations or the surrounding brush piles. I'm not 100 percent sure if the feeders are filled all year, but the watering stations are kept flowing year-round.

Prior to the addition of the bird blind, I birded from the campgrounds and fishing pier. During the fall and winter the lake hosts more than fifteen species of water-fowl, including American Wigeons, Northern Shovelers, Canada Geese, Hooded Mergansers, and Redheads. I'm always impressed with how good the birding is during October and November when the woods and fields are alive with Verdins, American Goldfinches, Cedar Waxwings, Vermilion Flycatchers, and a variety of sparrows. Summer is a good time to get a campsite and watch for Black-chinned Hummingbirds; I've found several tiny nests in the shrubs surrounding the campground.

Greater Roadrunner: A group of roadrunners is called a marathon or race, which makes sense because they can run up to fifteen miles per hour. They don't hang out in flocks too often, but they do pair up during breeding season. The male will present a selected female with a gift of a lizard, snake, or other fresh kill. If she accepts him, she will take the gift. If she rejects him, she will reject the gift and leave him standing alone in the field wondering why his gift wasn't good enough. The Greater Roadrunner is the state bird of New Mexico.

FIGURE 5.16. Greater Roadrunner (photo by Jennifer L. Bristol).

FIGURE 5.17. Greater Roadrunner taking a dust bath (photo by Jennifer L. Bristol).

Inks Dam National Fish Hatchery (228 species)
345 Clay Young Road, Burnet, TX 78611
https://www.fws.gov/southwest/fisheries/inks_dam/
Parking Lot, Short Trails, Bird Blinds

The National Fish Hatchery next door to Inks Lake State Park attracts a variety of shorebirds, ducks, and raptors to the fish breeding ponds. During the summer the ponds and nearby fields produce a variety of insects that the Barn Swallows are hungry for. From late spring to fall the massive pecan, oak, and cypress trees that live between the ponds and the river fill with White-eyed and Bell's Vireos, Verdins, Orchard Orioles, Painted Buntings, and Summer Tanagers. It seems that there is always an Osprey circling overhead looking for a juicy fish.

My husband and I traveled from Austin to see a Long-tailed Duck that was reported in the Travis Audubon Rare Bird Alert. We drove up to the parking lot, said hello to the staff member passing by, and Thomas excitedly asked where we might see the fabled duck. He responded with, "Um, you mean that duck?" and pointed to the only bird on the pond.

The duck was dawdling along the calm waters of the pond just feet from the parking lot, surrounded by bird nerds like ourselves. The bird was perfectly still and lovely, but in my excitement I took only shaky, overexposed photos. It's always good to conduct a self-check and a gear check before entering into an exciting birding experience.

There is a bird blind that has a drip and several feeders located in the woods opposite the ponds that is worth checking out. During the spring the feeders and drips bring in Painted and Indigo Buntings, Black-throated Sparrows, a variety of warblers, and three types of doves.

The fish hatchery was built in 1938 as part of the Public Works Administration to provide fish to the newly created lakes along the Colorado River. Then-congressman Lyndon B. Johnson orchestrated the agreement, which included construction of the facilities by the National Youth Administration.

Cedar Waxwing: The Cornell Lab of Ornithology "All About Birds" states that this bird is "a treat to find in your binocular view field." I wholeheartedly agree. I refer to Cedar Waxwings as the "cool kids," as they sport a distinctive black mask that look like sunglasses and can often be found hanging out in large groups. They are voracious fruit eaters and will eat the entire fruit, including the seeds. This behavior also makes them a master of distributing seeds, including those of invasive plants. Occasionally they will chow down on fermented berries or fruit that can cause them to become drunk and stumble around on the ground.

FIGURE 5.18. Cedar Waxwing (photo by Jennifer L. Bristol).

Pedernales Falls State Park (240 species)

2585 Park Road 6026, Johnson City, TX 78636
https://tpwd.texas.gov/state-parks/pedernales-falls
Parking Lot, Bird Blind, Short Trail

I have hiked almost every trail in this park, many of them several times. The best birding is near the parking areas, campgrounds, and the well-maintained bird blind. Take a moment to do a little birding at the visitor center when you check in; the overlook is down a short trail just off the parking lot. You might see woodpeckers, swifts, swallows, sparrows, or hummingbirds whizzing through the rugged cedar breaks or hawks drifting by on the thermals.

Motor to the bird blind during the spring and fall migration, and be prepared to be delighted. The sign out front says to keep your voices low when entering the bird blind area, which is a hard rule for my loud-talking, loud-laughing family to follow, but we do our best.

During our birding competitions, the blind has always produced for us. Painted Buntings, Scarlet Tanagers, Lark Sparrows, and warblers stop here for food and water during the spring migration, especially during drier years. The blind is beautifully maintained by the park hosts and has two drips and a picturesque flower garden: Woodhouse's Scrub-Jays, White-winged and Mourning Doves, Northern Cardinals, and Carolina Chickadees are year-round residents that frequent the gardens. One eBird post on July 7, 2017, reported a sighting of forty-seven species in the park on that day; in other words, the residents during the spring and summer months are plentiful.

Three of my favorite Hill Country birds live around the Pedernales Falls Overlook parking lot and trail. Get out of your car and start listening for the call of the endangered Golden-cheeked Warbler; males sing primarily from March to May. The song sounds remarkably like the tune "La Cucaracha." Walk approximately twenty yards down the trail, and look into the lacework of mature oaks and cedars to spy the distinct, flamboyant male warbler singing while perched near the top of a tree. The park is one of the few nesting habitats left in Central Texas for these birds. The treetops are also filled with the proud-looking Blue-gray Gnatcatchers, tiny birds that resemble miniature mockingbirds and are equally fierce at defending their territory. At the overlook, keep your ears open for the melodic, tumbling song of the Canyon Wren.

The parking lot at the trailhead for the Overlook Trail was one of our last stops on one of our six-day birding competitions. We strolled back to the parking lot after notching the Golden-cheeked Warbler and Canyon Wren when my husband pointed at a dead tree full of gray birds and whispered, "What are those?" I was dog tired and glanced at the birds, "Those are just more damn doves. They are really big here." My mom strode forward and laughed, "Doves? You need to get your eyes checked. Look again." The birds were a roost of approximately ten Mississippi Kites who looked back at me with disdain for having called them doves.

I have yet to see or hear a Wild Turkey in the park either from the campground, parking lots, or trails, even though they are common here. That's the thrill of birding: there is always something new to see.

≫ **Feather Fact** ≪

Canyon Wren: It is easier to hear the Canyon Wren than see it. Listen for the distinctive cascading call around canyons and cliffs of the Edwards Plateau, the Southwest, and Mexico. Canyon Wrens have a low center of gravity and big feet, which make it easy for them to scoot around boulders to search for insects. They get all the fluids they need from the insects they consume and rarely drink water. Their beak is located high on their narrow head, an adaptation that makes it possible for them to thrust their head into crevices to snatch a meal.

FIGURE 5.19. Canyon Wren in a rare still moment (photo by Jennifer L. Bristol).

Lady Bird Johnson Wildflower Center (150 species)

4801 La Crosse Avenue, Austin, TX 78739
https://www.wildflower.org
Parking Lot, Nature Center Campus, Short Trails

There is elegance to this space that only seems fitting as it bears the name of the former first lady and first-rate conservationist Lady Bird Johnson. The center's main purpose is to research native plants and promote their use across the state and nation; however, it has also become a place for families to bring their children to play and connect with nature at the Luci and Ian Family Garden.

Because of the carefully restored prairies a passel of sparrows arrives in the fall and stays until the spring: Chipping, Field, Harris's, Lincoln's, Savannah, and Vesper Sparrows can all be found darting in and out of the shrubs and grasses. The abundance of flowering plants brings in the Black-chinned and Ruby-throated Hummingbirds from April to September. Since there is not a large body of water on the property, you won't find waterfowl or shorebirds here, but you will find the Great Horned Owl during March and April. For several years a pair of owls has nested on the arch above the entrance to the center.

The center is a delight to visit in all seasons, with the best birding to be found at the Mollie Steves Zachary Texas Arboretum. The center is a great place to find information about which native plants are best for your ecoregion to attract the birds to your yard, school, church, or place of business. The more I learn about birds, the more I understand the value and need for native plants.

≫ **Feather Fact** ≪

Great-tailed Grackle: This iridescent black-and-purple social bird can be found throughout Texas except in the far east and west. Prior to the 1960s these birds were not common in Texas, but as agriculture and development expanded, so did their northern range. They are constantly chattering to each other in loud, cackling calls: it is one of the sounds I most associate with my home city of Austin. In the winter they gather in the evenings by the hundreds on power lines or roost trees. When feeding, they can mostly be found strutting along the lawns of parks, neighborhoods, school campuses, or parking lots searching for bugs, tidbits of trash, frogs, or little lizards.

FIGURE 5.20. Male Great-tailed Grackle (photo by Jennifer L. Bristol).

Copperfield Nature Trail (167 species)
1425 East Yager Lane, Austin, TX 78753
https://www.copperfieldtrails.org
Parking Lot, Short Trail

This is a fairly small urban park with a lot to offer. Tucked away in a magnificent oak forest on the edge of the Edwards Plateau and Blackland Prairies, this park follows a tributary watershed down to Walnut Creek. The trees and open spaces around the parking area off Yager Lane are decent, but if you venture a little farther down the ADA-accessible nature trail to the pond, the birding gets even better. The mix of live oaks, walnut, and Ashe juniper trees offers plenty of shelter and insects for migrating and resident birds alike; the trees also offer a nice canopy of shade to linger under during the warmer months. There are benches by the pond where you can sit and enjoy the birds.

The resident birds here can also be found at most Austin area locations and include Northern Cardinals, Blue Jays, House Finches, Red-bellied Woodpeckers, Carolina Wrens, and a local Red-shouldered Hawk. The spring migration gets hopping in mid-April as Common Yellowthroat and Nashville, Magnolia, and Yellow Warblers all filter through, feeding off the emerging worm and insect populations residing in the oak and walnut canopy. From May until September Western Kingbirds, White-eyed Vireos, Green Herons, and Yellow-crown Night-Herons call the park home. Because of the proximity to the neighborhood and abundant chimneys and birdhouses, Purple Martins and Chimney Swifts are also frequent flyers over the ponds and woodlands of the park.

I enjoy the birding most at the park from October to March when the winter birds return to mix it up with the year-round residents. Flocks of Cedar Waxwings descend on the juniper trees to feast on their berries while Hermit Thrushes, American Robins, and Spotted Towhees scratch through the leaf litter under the massive trees. White-throated, Chipping, Lincoln's, Field, and at least ten other types of sparrows can be found in the shrubs and grasses near the parking area and all along the nature trail, while Turkey and Black Vultures soar overhead. Of course, no bird walk in Austin is ever without the presence of the Great-tailed Grackle, and this park has a healthy resident population.

Walnut Creek is one of the longer watersheds in the Austin area as it snakes along the edge of the Edwards Plateau and Blackland Prairies. There are several parks along the watershed that also offer good birding and an escape into nature from the ever-growing metropolis of Austin.

⫸ Feather Fact ⫷

Lesser Goldfinch: This yellow-and-black little bird is as pretty to see as it is to hear. Lesser Goldfinches have a high, cheerful song that can often incorporate sounds from other birds. They prefer seeds from the sunflower family but will also eat thistle and other seeds, which makes it easy to attract them to feeders. Their range includes the southwestern part of the United States into Mexico and all the way south to Peru; however, they do not migrate long distances. They can be found across Texas except in parts of the Panhandle and Piney Woods.

FIGURE 5.21. Lesser Goldfinches on the feeder in February (photo by Jennifer L. Bristol).

Highland Mall ACC Campus and Capital Plaza Parking Lots
5600 North Interstate Highway 35, Austin, TX 78723
https://travisaudubon.org/purple-martin-parties
Parking Lot

Travis Audubon hosts Purple Martin parties during mid-July as the birds begin to congregate before heading to South America for the winter. Travis Audubon Society describes the event as "a hurricane of birds as hundreds of thousands of Purple Martins swirl into their roosting site each evening." While they are most commonly at the old Highland Mall or Capital Plaza parking lots, they do change location from time to time based on construction or other factors; please check the website for current events. The birds will congregate until late August, and then, poof, they are gone.

In a city known for its Mexican free-tailed bats, this is a second urban wildlife event that people can easily enjoy. The parties bring in dozens of viewers every evening to watch the birds twist and turn in their ancient ritual. The trees that remain in the parking lot offer a protected refuge for the birds to spend a restful night out of harm's way from predators or owls.

The birds start coming to their communal roosts at dusk after a day of eating millions of insects around the city. Common Nighthawks often accompany them as they snatch up bugs from around the streetlights. The streetlights are also a good place to look for the Monk Parakeets, which have flourished in the Austin area after being released. These bright green birds are quite industrious and will build large nests in streetlights and telephone poles where they live in large, talkative family units.

Houston Audubon Society offers similar viewing parties called Martin Migration Madness. Both Travis Audubon and Houston Audubon host informative and engaging field trips, speaker series, volunteer work days, and guided walks throughout the year. Both also own several sanctuaries that help conserve critical habitats for nesting and migratory birds.

⫸ **Feather Fact** ⫷

Purple Martin: This bird is an expert flyer that eats and drinks exclusively on the wing. Purple Martins are social birds that prefer to nest in groups and migrate in even larger groups. Roosts can get so large that they can be seen on Doppler radar as the birds emerge in the mornings to start their day of feeding on insects. Native Americans started placing hollowed-out gourds for them to nest in thousands of years ago, and humans in eastern and southern parts of North America have continued that tradition. They are one of three birds that nest only in houses built specifically for them by humans. Long-distance migrants, they will often cross the Gulf of Mexico in a single flight as they head north from South America.

FIGURE 5.22. Purple Martins coming in to roost in July (photo by Jennifer L. Bristol).

6 • San Antonio and the Western Edwards Plateau

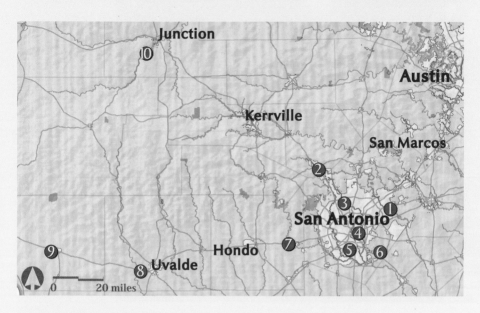

SAN ANTONIO AND THE WESTERN EDWARDS PLATEAU REGION

KEY:

1   Crescent Bend Nature Park
2   Cibolo Nature Center and Farm
3   Phil Hardberger Park and Urban Ecology Center
4   San Antonio Botanical Garden
5   Mitchell Lake Audubon Center
6   Calaveras Lake
7   Castroville Regional Park
8   Cook's Slough Sanctuary and Nature Park
9   Fort Clark Springs
10 South Llano River State Park

FIGURE 6.1.
Black-and-white
Warbler (photo by
Jennifer L. Bristol).

FIGURE 6.2. Carolina Chickadee (photo by Jennifer L. Bristol).

The city of San Antonio sits on the edge of several ecoregions: the Edwards Plateau, Blackland Prairies, South Texas Plains, and a dash of the Post Oak Savannah tossed in for good measure. Staying within a two-hour drive of San Antonio, this chapter also includes birding locations in Castroville, Brackettville, and Junction.

The once-shallow sea laid down layers of limestone that define the region with rolling rocky hills dotted with juniper and oak forests. Crystal-clear creeks and rivers flow through the region, making it a nature tourism destination for birding, kayaking, canoeing, tubing, hiking, and fishing. Even the early Spanish missionaries knew they had found a special place when they wandered into the area and set up missions along the San Antonito and Nueces Rivers. The birds know it is a special place as well.

FIGURE 6.3. Black-necked Stilt (photo by Thomas Nilles).

Crescent Bend Nature Park (252 species)
12805 Schaefer Road, Schertz, TX 78108
https://friendscbnp.zenfolio.com
Parking Lots, Short Trails, Bird Blinds

This relatively new park opened in 2009 and was once a residential neighborhood that was badly damaged in the hundred-year floods in 1997 and 1998. It is now jointly managed by Bexar County and the City of Schertz with support from the volunteers of Friends of Crescent Bend Nature Park.

Nestled along the banks of Cibolo Creek and on the edge of the Blackland Prairies, the small 170-acre park has become an excellent place to find common, migrant, and even rare birds. The nature park has a short 1.3-mile crushed-granite walking trail, a handful of picnic tables, two bird blinds, and restrooms that are all well maintained. The bird blinds are just a few yards from the parking area, and both have feeders and drips to draw in the birds. The blinds also fill with other really nice birders who are willing to share what they've seen that day. If you walk a little farther down the trail to the big pecan grove, there is an abundance of woodpeckers and flycatchers moving up and down the trees.

Down by the creek you might find a few ducks or shorebirds, but most likely they can be seen flying overhead to the little lake nearby. Resident birds include Great Blue Herons; Black-bellied Whistling Ducks; White-winged, Mourning, and Inca Doves; Red-shouldered Hawks; and Killdeer. April and May bring in a big variety of insect eaters such as Olive-sided, Yellow-bellied, Willow, Least, and Great Crested Flycatchers. The park also welcomes Black-throated Green, Magnolia, and Yellow Warblers; American Redstarts; and Rose-breasted Grosbeaks. During the fall Harris's, Lincoln's, Vesper, White-throated, and twelve other species of sparrows frequent the grasses and shrubs of the park. The mighty Barred Owl is a resident of the park, and its distinct *who cooks for you* can be heard in the evenings.

The friends group has a website that offers an excellent array of photos to help identify birds that frequent the park.

Crested Caracara: Otherwise known as the "Mexican Eagle," this bird is neither an eagle nor a hawk but a very large falcon. However, it doesn't act like a falcon. Crested Caracaras, as vultures do, prefer to eat carrion but are also known to wade into water to catch a fish or swoop down to snatch a rabbit. Unlike other falcons, they build nests and will return to those nests year after year. They can often be seen walking or even running along the ground while searching for their favorite prey. They do not migrate and can live up to twenty years, with most of that spent in the same territory and family group.

FIGURE 6.4. Crested Caracara with a meal (photo by Jennifer L. Bristol).

Cibolo Nature Center and Farm (232 species)

140 City Park Road, Boerne, TX 78006
http://www.cibolo.org
Parking Lot, Nature Center Campus, Short Trails

The center is set along the banks of Cibolo Creek, which originates in Boerne and traverses one hundred miles before emptying into the San Antonio River. There are a variety of trails to choose from to wander through the fields or enjoy the tranquility of the creek. The birding here is good year-round, and the knowledgeable staff offer guided birding walks for all ages and in all seasons.

On a sunny day in November we were treated to more than nine types of sparrows feeding in the restored prairie area and among the native plants around the nature center. Chipping, Vesper, Savannah, Lincoln's, and Swamp Sparrows, plus Dark-eyed Juncos, all enjoyed the warm sun after several weeks of rain.

During the summer months it is common to find Purple Martins darting back and forth to their house to feed their young. Summer is also a good time to see Painted Buntings, Barn Swallows, Western Kingbirds, and even a Yellow-billed Cuckoo or two. Spring of course brings waves of passerines, including raptors such as Mississippi Kites and Zone-tailed and Swainson's Hawks. Some of the more common year-round species include Golden-fronted and Ladder-backed Woodpeckers, Eastern Phoebes, Carolina Chickadees, and Black-crested Titmice.

The center itself is a great example of what a handful of passionate people can do to conserve nature and heritage in a rapidly growing community. Carolyn Chipman Evans, Brent Evans, and other citizens worked with the City of Boerne to preserve the land along the creek, and in 1990 they opened the center to the public. Since that time they have offered visitors a place to engage with nature and the rich cultural history of the Texas Hill County.

⋙ Feather Fact ⋘

Barn Swallow: This bird is an agile flyer with a forked tail that sets it apart from other swallows. Barn Swallows build their nests exclusively in and on human-made structures instead of the caves they once occupied. They are also the most widespread swallow in the Americas and will nest in most of North America, including Texas, and winter in Central and South America. When they sit still for a moment, it is easier to see just how brilliant their colors are with rich blues, a rust-colored throat, buff belly, and gray wings. Their beautiful colors and shape of their feathers caught the eye of the hat makers in the 1800s, and their populations were ravaged for the sake of fashion. Protected under the Migratory Bird Treaty Act in 1918, the birds have made a comeback and the populations are stable.

FIGURE 6.5. Barn Swallow on old ranch fence (photo by Jennifer L. Bristol).

Phil Hardberger Park and Urban Ecology Center (132 species)
13203 Blanco Road, San Antonio, TX 78216 (Park East) and 8400 NW Military Highway, San Antonio, TX 78230 (Park West)
https://www.philhardbergerpark.org/index.php and https://www.philhardbergerpark.org/park-west/urban-ecology-center
Parking Lot, Nature Center Campus, Short Trail

Former mayor of San Antonio Phil Hardberger valued open spaces and the rugged nature of Bexar County. He helped distinguish San Antonio as one of the most livable cities in the United States by increasing access to natural spaces for all citizens throughout the city. The park that bears his name is the crown jewel in the "green necklace" that now encircles San Antonio.

The 330-acre park was a former dairy farm and today serves as a place for learning, recreating, and relaxing. The birding isn't extraordinary here but can be counted on for the local favorites. The savanna restoration area attracts a good variety of sparrows during the winter months. There are two ways to explore the savanna: take the short walk on the crushed-granite trail around the edge or pull up a chair and sit on the deck of the Ecology Center. Chipping, Field, Lark, Lincoln's, and White-throated Sparrows can all be found dancing in and out of the little bluestem grasses of the savanna. A few more small brown birds such as the Bewick's, Carolina, and House Wrens also frequent the field and oak mottes.

The giant oaks have provided food and shelter for passerines for centuries and are always a good place to look for buntings, warblers, and vireos during the spring and fall. During the winter months small birds such as Cedar Waxwings, Golden-crowned and Ruby-crowned Kinglets, Blue-gray Gnatcatchers, and American Goldfinches can be found darting through the massive trees. The raised boardwalk that juts out from the center is a good place to watch for Barn Swallows, Chimney Swifts, and Purple Martins during the summer months. The raised walk follows one of the water conservation systems for about one hundred yards, which makes it a good vantage point to watch for insect-catching birds.

The Ecology Center has nice restrooms and a few stone picnic tables if you want to spend several relaxing hours birding. The birding from the parking lots is also good year-round. Summer Tanagers nest in the park during the summer and can often be seen and heard from the parking area.

This park will soon be connected to the adjacent park property via a land bridge that people and wildlife can utilize. The bridge will cross Wurzbach Parkway and should be completed in 2020.

White-winged Dove: This bird, which seems so abundant now, was once down to just around five hundred thousand birds. In the 1920s and 1930s heavy agriculture (especially in the Rio Grande Valley) reduced the traditional nesting habitats by 90 percent. Overhunting also reduced the populations; however, through conservation efforts and regulated hunting the birds have made a comeback and are thriving. Their range now covers most of Texas and Mexico. By the 1980s the birds started expanding their range and can now be found as far north as Maine in limited numbers. I love to hear them cooing during the spring in my yard in Austin.

FIGURE 6.6. White-winged Dove on a cold winter morning (photo by Jennifer L. Bristol).

San Antonio Botanical Garden (247 species)
555 Funston Place, San Antonio, TX 78209
http://www.sabot.org
Parking Lot, Nature Center Campus, Short Trail

My granny lived in San Antonio for a short while when I was young, and she liked to take us to the Botanical Garden to wander around. I always thought the strange glass and metal structures looked like something out of Star Wars; I still think they do.

The Botanical Garden was once the source of an artesian spring and still has many fountains and water features that attract the birds throughout the year. The center used to be a more traditional botanical garden but has since expanded to embrace Texas native plants and include education about water and habitat conservation. There are a multitude of looping trails that wind their way through a variety of micro ecoregions that attract a wide variety of birds. There are several good stops along the way, and I recommend spending time in the bird-watch structure or along the small pond in the northern part of the garden.

Since there is a pond, the garden brings in a few ducks such as Northern Shovelers, Ring-necked Ducks, and American Coots. In December, the ground gets hopping with American Robins, Curve-billed and Long-billed Thrashers, Hermit Thrushes, Spotted Towhees, and Northern Cardinals. As you meander down the trails, you might come across a tai chi or yoga class quietly flexing their muscles while their minds unwind in the tranquility of nature.

April and May are the best months to pack a lunch and spend the day milling around the garden to enjoy the splendor of the spring migration. Prothonotary Warblers, Summer Tanagers, Blue Grosbeaks, and American Redstarts are just the tip of the iceberg of migratory birds that stop over at this lush urban park. More than eighteen species of warblers and seven species of vireos pass through the garden in April alone. If you visit in April and May, you might want to study up on identifying flycatchers, as the park fills with them during this time.

On a rare occasion endangered Golden-cheeked Warblers will stop by as they make their way along the Edwards Plateau looking for a safe place to nest among the Ashe junipers and live oak forests of the limestone hills north of San Antonio. Government Canyon State Natural Area is the best place to find the endangered birds in the San Antonio area.

Aside from looking like a *Star Wars* set, the garden is lovely in all seasons. In 2017, an additional two acres were added to include the Family Adventure Garden, where children can play, explore, and connect with nature.

Ruby-throated Hummingbird: This tiny bird crosses the Gulf of Mexico in a single flight when it migrates from Central and South America to North America by way of Texas. In recent years some enterprising birds have taken up residence year-round along the Texas Gulf Coast. Changing weather patterns and human-supported year-round flowering plants allow them to survive in the area. They are one of the few birds that can fly both backward and forward and hover. They get their name from the red-colored, iridescent feathers located on a male's throat that flash red when it whizzes by. They are the only hummingbirds that breed in eastern North America.

FIGURE 6.7. Male Ruby-throated Hummingbird (photo by Jennifer L. Bristol).

Mitchell Lake Audubon Center (345 species)
10750 Pleasanton Road, San Antonio, TX 78221
http://mitchelllake.audubon.org
Parking Lot, Nature Center Campus, Short Trails, Driving Tour

I really want to like the Mitchell Lake Audubon Center. I stubbornly keep walking the trails and the roads thinking I will find more birds. But I'm wrong—again and again. Don't be a fool like me. The secret to the center is to park in the parking lot, pay the entrance fee, bird the grounds near the visitor center, and then take the three-mile driving tour around the treatment ponds and lake. You will see an abundance of birds around the ponds from your car. In addition to more than forty migratory shorebirds there are other species such as Least and Western Sandpipers, Long-billed Dowitchers, Stilt Sandpipers, Killdeer, and Black-necked Stilts that call the calm, shallow waters of the ponds home year-round.

My husband and I walked the entire campus for hours one hot day in April, and it truly is a bounty of birds. By the time we reached Basin 3, my husband sarcastically proclaimed, "It's a good thing we are already married. I'm questioning your sanity at this point." It's not easy schlepping around a bunch of cameras and optics in the heat of South Texas. Thankfully, by midday kettles of passing hawks and vultures, shorebirds of all kinds, American White Pelicans, and ducks all show up in abundance. There was a Dickcissel in every tall bush.

The moral of that story is that to maintain your marital bliss, take the driving tour if you have more than five pounds of gear. Or better yet, take one of the guided tours the center offers. The staff and volunteers have done a great job restoring the native scrub and prairie habitat, which is quickly disappearing from the south side of San Antonio.

The center has limited hours that change with the seasons, so please check the website before visiting. I've shown up when the gates were already closed for the day, which is no fun.

⇒ Feather Fact ⇐

Long-billed Dowitcher: This bird puts the *long* in long-distance migration and bills. Long-billed Dowitchers winter in South Texas, Florida, and Mexico but will travel all the way to Siberia and the Arctic Circle to breed. The females incubate the eggs, but once the chicks hatch, the males take over caring for the young. Because these birds cover such an expansive range, it is difficult for researchers to get a good estimate of their populations; with that said, they do seem to be abundant along the Gulf Coast and South Texas during the winter. When they are feeding, they bob up and down like a sewing-machine needle as they work their long bill into the mudflats.

FIGURE 6.8. Long-billed Dowitcher (photo by Thomas Nilles).

Calaveras Lake (250 species)

12991 Bernhardt Road, San Antonio, TX 78263
https://www.cpsenergy.com/en/about-us/community/lakes-and-parks/braunig-calaveras-lakes.html
Parking Lots, Campground, Short Trail

This lake has parking lots galore to bird from. My husband, four dogs, and I visited in late November and counted up to twenty-five species in an hour without much effort. Birding with the dogs is a little tricky since they pull on the leashes and make it hard to focus the optics.

We first stopped in the ridiculously large boat ramp parking area located near the entrance of the park and checked out the cove to the north. The cove was filled with the most Pied-billed Grebes I have ever seen in one place. The lake also hosts Eared and Western Grebes from November to March. At the cove we saw Neotropic Cormorants, Great and Snowy Egrets, Mallards, and a Great Blue Heron. The large hackberry and mesquite trees were filled with Yellow-rumped Warblers, Ruby-crowned Kinglets, Red-winged Blackbirds, Northern Cardinals, and an easygoing Vermilion Flycatcher that seemed to enjoy having his picture taken.

As we walked to the point of the first cove, an Osprey dove out of the sky to catch a fish. His success in catching his prey caused the gentleman fishing nearby to exclaim, "I wish I had his luck; nothing's biting over here." The majority of visitors on that after-noon seemed to be fishermen. By noon, the parking lot was full of father-son groups who had escaped the drudgery of Black Friday shopping. I have to admit, I'm not sure I would want to eat a fish from the lake, considering it is a cooling pond for the CPS Energy Coal Plant; hopefully they were just catching and releasing. CPS Energy owns and manages Calaveras and Braunig Lakes. Braunig Lake is also a good birding spot and is an easy twenty-minute drive to the west.

We motored along the paved road to check out some of the other coves and parking areas, all of which provided easy access to a variety of birds. Kansas Cove had a nice day-use area with an ADA walkway that connects to a large fishing pier. From the peer we could easily see into the cove and view the surrounding trees. American White Pelicans floated about, mixing it up with Redheads and American Coots.

This isn't a great place to look for warblers, but the grasses and shrubs fill with more than fifteen species of sparrows in the fall along with Bewick's, Carolina, House, and Marsh Wrens. The Loggerhead Shrike is a year-round resident that I never get tired of watching as it impales its prey on sticks or barbed wire.

This is a major recreation lake for San Antonio and might be too busy for birding in the summer. The best birding seems to start in late summer and continues until mid-April.

❧ Feather Fact ❧

Pied-billed Grebe: This compact aquatic-loving bird can be found year-round in Texas on most ponds or lakes. The birds dive underwater to feed on crustaceans and fish or to make a quick getaway from a predator. Like other grebes, Pied-billeds eat their own feathers to line their intestines to protect against the harsh shells and bones they consume. They prefer to build their nests on floating plants or other floating objects, which is one reason they also prefer the still waters of ponds and lakes to those of rivers.

FIGURE 6.9. Pied-billed Grebe (photo by Thomas Nilles).

Castroville Regional Park (216 species)

816 Alsace Avenue, Castroville, TX 78009
https://castrovilletx.gov/2346/Castroville-Regional-Park
Parking Lot, Wastewater Treatment Facility, Campground, Short Trail

Tucked in along the banks of the Medina River, this local 126-acre park offers some great year-round birding. A trail that loops the park will take visitors on a journey to all the gems the location has to offer.

During the winter and early spring the pond and wastewater treatment facility bring in the shorebirds and ducks, while the fields bring in the sparrows. Near the entrance is a pollinator garden that the Black-chinned and Ruby-throated Humming-birds frequent. A parade of color flashes through the trees along the river during April and May. Bullock's, Hooded, and Scott's Orioles all pass through along with Blue Grosbeaks, Painted and Indigo Buntings, Northern Parulas, and Summer Tanagers. Evening visitors might catch a glimpse of a Great Horned, Barn, or Barred Owl or even a Yellow-crowned Night-Heron.

Located about thirty miles west of San Antonio, the little town of Castroville has an interesting history and is known as the "Little Alsace of Texas."

> ### ≫ Feather Fact ≪
>
> **Double-crested Cormorant:** This fishing bird can be found in both freshwater and saltwater wetlands across most of North America, with high concentrations wintering in Texas. These cormorants sit low in the water like loons when they are on the surface and will dive deep to catch a fish with their long, hooked beak. Unlike most waterbirds they lack high concentrations of preen oils, which help shed water; look for them perched on rocks or stumps with their wings extended to dry. Listen for them making a deep, bullfrog-like sound when they are congregating. For the most part they are drab brown birds with a patch of yellow or orange skin around the beak and jewel-like green eyes. Since the ban on the pesticide DDT, these birds have made a strong comeback.

FIGURE 6.10. Double-crested Cormorant drying its wings (photo by Thomas Nilles).

Cook's Slough Sanctuary and Nature Park (281 species)
Uvalde County Road 106, Uvalde, TX 78801
https://www.visituvalde.com/uvalde_attractions/cooks-slough-sanctuary-and-nature-park/
Parking Lot, Wastewater Treatment Facility, Short Trail

I've explored the sanctuary only once, and I really liked it. My mother and I stopped by in late December on our way to Marfa for New Year's and happened upon a large squadron of American White Pelicans feeding and grooming themselves in a lazy, carefree way.

The sanctuary is outside Uvalde along the banks of Cook's Slough and the wastewater treatment facilities. The parking lot is small and did not offer the best birding, but the short, elevated walkway makes it easy to access the ponds. The shallow ponds are filled with fish and frogs just waiting to be snatched up by the eagerly awaiting herons and egrets that stand ready around the perimeters.

There is a large outdoor classroom/pavilion that overlooks the islands on one of the ponds that is a great space where you can escape the heat and watch the warblers move through the substantial oak trees on one side and the waterfowl and shorebirds on the other. The trails that wind around the ponds are wide and flat with two shaded benches where birders can sit and observe.

The ponds bring in the ducks and shorebirds, but it also offers one of the more northern points for several South Texas birds such as Green Jays, Great Kiskadees, Couch's Kingbirds, Cactus Wrens, and even Groove-billed Anis, which inhabit the twenty-five-acre nature park. Some of the raptors spotted in the area include Zone-tailed, Swainson's, Harris's, Red-tailed, and Red-shouldered Hawks.

April and May are great times to visit the area. The flowers are in bloom, and the trees and fields are thick with migrating birds. Blue Grosbeaks, Summer Tanagers, Painted Buntings, Bullock's Orioles, and Yellow Warblers all add to the grand colors of spring, while Scissor-tailed Flycatchers, Western Kingbirds, and Vermilion Flycatchers launch from the treetops to snatch a bug or perform a mating dance.

If you visit during the spring, remember to take your bug spray; the warblers, swallows, and flycatchers eat a lot of bugs but not all of them! There are no restrooms at this location. Garner State Park is just north of Uvalde and is also a lovely spot to bird during the week when the park is not so busy.

Blue Grosbeak: This splendid blue bird has a summer range that includes Texas. Blue Grosbeaks can be found feeding along the ground for insects and seeds that they easily crack with their cone-shaped bills. The birds that summer along the eastern part of North America will fly over the Gulf of Mexico during migration, while the western breeding birds will travel overland. Blue Grosbeaks often line their nests with snakeskins. It is thought that they do this to ward off predators, but they might do so because snakeskins are long and easy to shape.

FIGURE 6.11. Male Blue Grosbeak (photo by Thomas Nilles).

Fort Clark Springs (242 species)
Swim Park Lane, Brackettville, TX 78832
https://www.fortclark.com
Parking Lots, Short Trails

Fort Clark was established in 1852 along the banks of Las Moras (the mulberries) Springs. I'm sure the fresh water, native pecans, and thriving wildlife was alluring to the US Army when they arrived to set up camp in late spring of 1852. The waters were also a favored resting spot for the Coahuiltecan, Apache, and Comanche. After the Anglos arrived, the fort was established to protect the road from San Antonio to El Paso, a journey that would have taken up to thirty days under favorable conditions. I shudder to think what additional misery unfavorable conditions would have included.

The pool is still used today and is a cherished spot to cool off during the summer. Julie Wernersbach and Carolyn Tracy tout the pool as one of their top-five favorite swimming spots in their fun book, *The Swimming Holes of Texas*. I agree with their sage assessment.

The birding in the parking lot from November to May is pretty darn great. The mature trees lining the banks of Las Moras Creek and the adjacent fields offer plenty of food and shelter for resident and migrating birds. The creek and wetlands are frequented by Mexican Ducks, Northern Shovelers, Gadwalls, and Pied-billed and Eared Grebes. The woods above the parking lot along Swim Park Lane are a good place to look for Long-billed Thrashers, Northern Cardinals, Hermit Thrushes, and other birds who enjoy picking through leaf litter of the scrub brush.

The cool water and nearby fields also bring in the bugs that are harvested by Black Phoebes; Couch's and Western Kingbirds; and Ash-throated, Brown-crested, and Vermilion Flycatchers. Smaller birds such as Blue-gray Gnatcatchers and Bell's, White-eyed, and Yellow-throated Vireos also feast on the variety of insects during the spring and early summer. A few of the resident birds include Lesser Goldfinches, Northern Mockingbirds, Cactus Wrens, Black-crested Titmice, Green Jays, and Great Kiskadees.

It's easy to while away the hours under the dappled sunlight coming through the canopy of cottonwoods as you look at the beautiful array of birds and listen to the soft sounds of flowing water and the rustling leaves.

﹥﹥ Feather Fact ﹤﹤

Blue-gray Gnatcatcher: This bird looks like a miniature Northern Mockingbird and often acts similarly. These gnatcatchers summer and nest in Central and North Texas where oak forests are plentiful. The range of this small bird has shifted farther north in the past decade, with some never leaving the coastal region. This shift is attributed to increasing temperatures over the past few decades. It is considered a short-range migrating bird that enjoys feeding on aphids, ants, bees, and moths. The little grayish birds are industrious nest builders and will construct as many as seven nests in a season. Look for them in the upper parts of the trees with their blue and white tails erect and in constant motion.

FIGURE 6.12. Blue-gray Gnatcatcher (photo by Thomas Nilles).

South Llano River State Park (265 species)
1927 Park Road 73, Junction, TX 76849
https://tpwd.texas.gov/state-parks/south-llano-river
Parking Lots, Campground, Short Trails, Bird Blinds

Get ready for a birding bonanza. The secret to this park's amazing parking lot birding is the variety of habitat easily accessible to visitors. The state park has four well-maintained bird blinds that are in close proximity to the parking lots or campgrounds. Each blind has drip and water features that mimic the landscape and ranching heritage of the area. It has six parking lots, a visitor center, a campground that is always full of fellow birders, and miles of hiking and biking trails.

More important, the 2,630-acre park preserves the complex layers of habitat needed to support this abundance of birds and wildlife. From the cedar breaks along the limestone hills to the riparian areas along the river, each system offers the birds the food, water, and shelter they require to raise their families or fuel up as they pass through during the migration seasons.

The visitor center/office parking lot should be your first stop. From April to September the hummingbirds buzz past excitedly as they move from the feeders to their perches. There are also Barn Swallows, Purple Martins, House Finches, flycatchers, and sparrows that dance through the air, perch on the fence, or scratch for bugs in the yard.

Just south of the visitor center is the parking area for the Fawn Trail and Agarita Bird Blind. The walk to the bird blind is short and full of birds darting in and out of the mesquite and juniper trees. During the spring, the blind and surrounding trees are bustling with Black-throated Sparrows, Painted Buntings, Inca Doves, and Blue-gray Gnatcatchers, and on one occasion we spotted a Scott's Oriole.

My mother and I met a wonderfully odd woman at the blind one April morning. The woman was attractive, fit, and dressed more like a runner than a birder. She was reluctant to chat, but my mother's southern charm eventually opened her up to a conversation. She finally revealed that she was on a two-month trip by herself to see as many birds, parks, and states as she could. Earlier in the year her last child had fledged and went off to college. The winter months in Wisconsin had been hard for her, and even harder was the realization that she and her husband of more than twenty years no longer had anything in common. Rather than feel sorry for herself, she took a sabbatical from her job, packed up her minivan, and hit the road for a little quality soul-searching time. We both commended her for finding solace in the birds and admitted we were a little envious of her two-month trip. My mother assured her that life goes on and even gets better after the kids go off on their own journeys. We wished her well as she jogged off down the trail in search of the Golden-cheeked Warbler.

The campground is full of birds and worth a stroll or drive-through. Several park hosts have feeders that attract Indigo Buntings, Golden-fronted Woodpeckers, Orchard Orioles, Northern Cardinals, and a variety of seedeaters. The campground is also full of chatty birders, both novice and skilled. If you walk through RV row, you might pick up some intel on what birds are being seen and where. The Acorn Bird Blind is just past campsite #43.

The parking lot for the walk-in campsites is worth noting. While birding with my mother, we scored twelve species of birds while we were getting our gear together at the truck. At the Juniper Bird Blind just off the parking lot we were treated to a Black-capped Vireo darting in for the world's fastest bath. The Nashville and Yellow Warblers and Lark, Field, and White-crowned Sparrows all took their time bathing in the shallow pools under the cool drip, but the Black-capped Vireo flashed down from the Ashe juniper tree, wet his wings, and was gone in a nanosecond. Of the twenty-plus photos I took of the brilliant black, buff, and green bird, only two turned out okay. Photo or no photo, I was thrilled to see the endangered bird and add it to my life list.

As a side note, my mother helped set aside thousands of acres of conservation lands in Texas to help protect the Black-capped Vireo and Golden-cheeked Warbler, and my father worked diligently to secure funding from sporting goods taxes for state parks like this one.

There is something magical and even romantic about the Windmill Bird Blind, which is flanked by an old barn and cedar-post fence that stand as a link to the ranching heritage of the area. The tin on the barn is rusted but not rotten. As the early-morning light filters through the trees, one can almost see the rancher saddling up his trusty horse; getting ready for a long, hot day of moving cattle; and mending fences.

Wild Turkeys gather in the field past the bird blind from October until April. The pasture is also a great place to see Northern Bobwhites and to look for resident sparrows such as Rufous-crowned, Field, Chipping, and Lark Sparrows. You can view the field from the parking lot by the river as well.

⫸ Feather Fact ⫷

Black-capped Vireo: This small black, buff, and green warbler was placed on the endangered species list in 1987 and delisted in 2018. Thanks to conservation efforts to manage the nesting habitats in Texas and Oklahoma, the birds have made a comeback even though they are still considered threatened by US Fish and Wildlife. Part of that conservation effort involved management of the parasitic Brown-headed Cowbird that laid eggs in the vireo's tiny nests. Males and females share the same plumage; however, mature males have an unusual reddish eye.

FIGURE 6.13. Male Black-capped Vireo (photo courtesy of Romey Swanson).

7 • Corpus Christi and the Coastal Bend

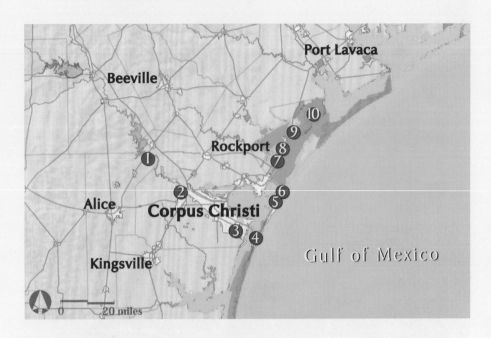

CORPUS CHRISTI AND THE COASTAL BEND REGION

KEY:

1   Lake Corpus Christi State Park
2   Hazel Bazemore County Park
3   Oso Bay Wetlands Preserve and Learning Center
4   Packery Channel Oak Motte Sanctuary
5   Port Aransas Nature Preserve at Charlie's Pasture
6   Leonabelle Turnball Birding Center
7   Connie Hagar Cottage Sanctuary
8   Rockport Beach Park
9   Goose Island State Park
10 Aransas National Wildlife Refuge

FIGURE 7.1 . Tricolored Heron fluffing his feathers (photo by Jennifer L. Bristol).

FIGURE 7.2. American Avocets (photo by Jennifer L. Bristol).

FIGURE 7.3. Blue-winged Warbler (photo by Jennifer L. Bristol).

FIGURE 7.4. Eastern Wood-Peewee (photo by Jennifer L. Bristol).

The Coastal Bend region is part of the Coastal Prairies and Marshes ecoregion that extends from Victoria to Kingsville and inland toward George West, with Corpus Christi at the center. The region is remarkably flat with remnants of tallgrass prairies, scrub, oak mottes, and endless agricultural fields stretched over the ancient sand dunes.

The region is also the terminus for several rivers, including the Colorado to the north, the Guadalupe and San Antonio in the middle, and the Nueces to the south. The rivers and their tributaries capture the thirty to fifty inches of rain that falls annually in the region and efficiently distribute it back into the water system. The fresh waters that flow from these mighty rivers fill the bays and estuaries that are the lifeblood for so many wintering, migratory, and year-round birds. The endangered Whooping Crane feeds on blue crabs found in San Antonio Bay from December to March. There are only a few hundred Whoopers left in the world, and it is a thrill to see these graceful birds in the wild along the Texas Coast.

The coast is also rimmed with barrier islands that shield the inland from hurricanes and storms. These low, narrow islands are also critical bird habitat. As the migrants cross the Gulf of Mexico in the spring, they are ready to alight on the first land they see to find food and fresh water. Often the islands are their salvation from the long journey across the open water.

This is also the home of the legendary 825,000-acre King Ranch. In addition to being one of the largest ranches in the world for more than 160 years, the hacienda is home to more than three hundred species of birds. Birding tours are offered for a fee, which I highly recommend if you have the time.

Lake Corpus Christi State Park (266 species)
23194 Park Road 25, Mathis, TX 78368
https://tpwd.texas.gov/state-parks/lake-corpus-christi
Parking Lots, Campgrounds, Short Trails, Bird Blind

This park, and the adjacent Girl Scout Camp, conserves one of the last remaining stands of brush country in the area. Most of the other surrounding properties are now agricultural lands, developed, or part of the lake. Just outside the town of Mathis, Lake Corpus Christi has been one of the largest artificial bodies of water in Texas since the mid-1930s. The lake supplies the more than four hundred thousand citizens of the Corpus Christi metro area with fresh water from the Nueces River. The brush country, along with the fresh water of the reservoir, makes the 365-acre park a wonderful place for neotropical birds to stop over during the migrations or spend the winter alongside many of the South Texas residents.

In 2017, the friends group of the park installed a bird blind with a drip and several feeding stations a few hundred yards from the CCC Refectory. However, before you go marching off to the bird blind, take a look around the pavilion and walk to the overlook. The yard and overlook are always good spots to see Green Jays, Ospreys, Cliff Swallows, and a surprising variety of gulls and terns. I like to imagine a Lipan Apache looking out from the bluff, considering the land and river that stretched out below. The oak trees surrounding the pavilion always seem to have White-eyed Vireos or Northern Cardinals chattering and dancing about them.

My husband and I camped in the Opossum Bend Camping Loop on Halloween one year. In the morning we took the dogs for a walk, and the bushes were covered in spider webs that had collected the morning dew, giving them the appearance of tiny threads of silver and diamonds that glistened in the South Texas sun. There were also thousands of butterflies and moths migrating through, which added an extra pop of color to the brush thickets.

Along the lake near the day-use picnic area, we saw Great Blue and Green Herons, Eared Grebes, Ruddy Ducks, Wilson's Snipes, and a Ringed Kingfisher. The park staff told us that the same area is a good place to see Upland and Spotted Sandpipers, Greater Yellowlegs, and Black-necked Stilts during late summer into early fall. In the mowed area we saw Inca and White-winged Doves, Common Ground-Doves, Lincoln's Sparrows, Killdeer, and a well-fed male Vermilion Flycatcher.

Late fall and winter are good times to visit when the weather is mild and dry and more than 120 species are present. If spring is your thing, then I recommend visiting between April and May when more than 150 species can be found at the park. When camping during the summer months, search the sultry evening skies for Common Nighthawks and Common Pauraques, and if you're lucky, you might be treated to the song of the Chuck-will's-widow.

⋙ Feather Fact ⋘

Inca Dove: This dove lives year-round in the US Southwest and Mexico. The feathers, which look like scales, keep the birds well camouflaged in the grasslands of the Southwest and Coastal Plains. Like me, they hate the cold. Since they do not migrate, they will huddle together on top of one another in pyramids to stay warm. As winters become milder, they have expanded their range north and seem to be well suited for living in and among suburban and urban areas. Like other doves, they feed their chicks a protein-rich liquid called "crop milk" that is formed in a pouch just above the parent's stomach and regurgitated. They have red eyes that turn an even deeper shade of red when they feel threatened.

FIGURE 7.5. Inca Dove (photo by Thomas Nilles).

Hazel Bazemore County Park (338 species)
4343 County Road 69, Corpus Christi, TX 78410
https://hawkwatch.org/migration/item/82-corpus-christi-hawkwatch
Parking Lots, Boardwalk, Bird Blind, Observation Platform

This is a very cool place to observe one of the wonders of nature: the fall hawk migration. Here at this seventy-seven-acre park located along a bend in the Nueces River just north of Corpus Christi, more than seven hundred thousand hawks pass by every year. Hawk watchers count the birds from August 1 to November 15 and record the daily numbers on a chart at the hawk watch tower. I'm impressed by the number of birds counted and how many birds the hawk watchers can spot in a day. What are hawk watchers? They are experienced birders who volunteer their time to count the passing birds and report their findings to Hawk Watch International, who uses the data to make the case for more conservation lands along the raptor flyways.

Broad-winged Hawks are the main feature of the fall migration; however, more than twenty-five other species of raptors sail past this point on their way to Central and South America. Broad-winged Hawks pass through this location by the thousands on their four thousand–mile journey; with a good tailwind they can travel almost seventy miles in a day. At this unique location, the Mississippi and Central Flyways converge as they follow the coastline into Mexico. The bluff above the river makes it easy to watch for approaching hawks and other migrating species.

Sometimes the hawk watch volunteers point out tiny specks in the sky and seem to know exactly what they are. To me, they look like specks in the sky. If I'm lucky, a hawk will thoughtfully come closer to the bluff so I can focus my optics enough to identify it. The trained volunteers watch carefully for subtle flight behaviors that help them quickly and accurately identify everything from Wood Storks to Cooper's Hawks.

Aside from the large raptors, the tiniest of birds also fly through during the spring and fall migrations. Black-chinned, Buff-bellied, Rufous, and Ruby-throated Hummingbirds frantically whiz by as they fuel up to complete their journeys.

It is easy to spend several hours at this park. Bring a chair and hang out on the hawk watch platform during the spring or fall, or bring a lunch and grab a picnic table down by the river to watch for Belted and Ringed Kingfishers, ducks, herons, flycatchers, and sparrows.

Broad-winged Hawk: Broad-winged Hawks are medium-sized raptors that enjoy flocking together. It is a thrill to look up in the South Texas skies and see a kettle of Broad-wings circling through a thermal to form a "river of raptors." Most birds only pass through Texas, while some will breed and nest in the forests of East Texas. Fossil records show that these hawks have lived in North America for more than four hundred thousand years. They feed on a wide range of amphibians, mammals, insects, and other birds, which makes them adaptive, and their populations have slightly increased over the past decade.

FIGURE 7.6. Broad-winged Hawk (photo courtesy of Greg Lasley; used with permission).

Oso Bay Wetlands Preserve and Learning Center (246 species)
2446 North Oso Parkway, Corpus Christi, Texas 78414
https://www.cctexas.com/services/general-government/oso-bay-wetlands-preserve-learning-center
Parking Lot, Nature Center Campus, Short Trails, Observation Platforms

Late November and early December are my favorite times to visit the Oso Bay Preserve. During these months the majestic Sandhill Cranes roost nearby and can be seen flying overhead in the late mornings or at dusk. Greater White-fronted and Snow Geese, Northern Pintails, and Mottled Ducks can also be found on the wing or on the bay.

However, April through June is actually the best time to visit to see the variety of birds the preserve has to offer. The trees around the parking lot make it easy to spot perching birds such as Eastern Phoebes, Loggerhead Shrikes, Painted Buntings, and Northern Mockingbirds. It is also common to see gulls and terns passing overhead from the parking lot. The fresh water and native plants surrounding the nature center bring in Black-throated Green Warblers, White-eyed Vireos, and Orchard and Baltimore Orioles during the spring.

One of the staff members documented a large flock of Wood Storks in early June, which I find exciting since I personally have yet to observe one in the wild. June is also a good time to see Buff-bellied, Ruby-throated, and Black-chinned Hummingbirds.

It is worthwhile to venture onto the paved and crushed-granite trails to one of the observation decks to look for ducks and shorebirds feeding in the shallow waters of Oso Bay. Two miles of ADA-friendly looping trails meander through the 162-acre park and take visitors on a journey through the scrub brush out to the bay. The habitat within the preserve provides enough resources to bring in a mix of resident South Texas birds, such as Great Kiskadees, Brown Thrashers, Pyrrhuloxias, Olive Sparrows, Inca Doves, and Groove-billed Anis.

I visited the center for the dedication of the giant heron sculpture at the entrance of the preserve in 2016. At that time, only a few homes existed across from the preserve. Fast-forward to just a few years later, and almost every lot surrounding the preserve has a new home on it. Conservation of large areas of habitat is critical for birds to nest, feed, and raise their families in this rapidly growing part of the country.

Mottled Duck: This medium-sized duck lives in fresh waters along the Gulf of Mexico from Florida to Mexico. While these ducks are commonly seen along the Texas coast, their populations are in sharp decline due to overhunting and habitat loss. Partners in Flight has moved them to its Red Watch List, which is the highest level of concern. They are closely related to Mallards and American Black Ducks, which they hybridize with frequently, another cause for population drops. Look for them dabbling in shallow fresh waters or waddling along the mudflats looking for plant matter, snails, beetles, and even dragonflies.

FIGURE 7.7. Mottled Duck and her chicks (photo by Jennifer L. Bristol).

Packery Channel Oak Motte Sanctuary (319 species)
14218 South Padre Island Drive, Corpus Christi, TX 78418
http://www.audubonoutdoorclub.com/packery
Parking Lots, Boardwalk

At first glance there doesn't seem to be much to the small Nueces County Park and adjacent Oak Motte Sanctuary. It seems to consist of one, big live oak motte with a boardwalk around the outer edge of the trees and a small field. However, those trees are important. According to the Audubon Outdoor Club, the trees are the only remaining stand of coastal oaks on the entire 113-mile Padre Island. During the spring migration the trees at both locations light up like Christmas trees with the bright colors of migrating warblers and orioles, including Blackpolls and Cerulean Warblers and Baltimore and Orchard Orioles.

Beyond the oak motte is a second boardwalk that overlooks a seasonal pond and fields filled with native vegetation such as bay laurel, lantana, mustang grapes, and coastal grasses. Yellow-crowned and Black-crowned Night-Herons, Green and Great Blue Herons, Snowy and Great Egrets, Greater Yellowlegs, and White Ibises frequent the pond when water is present.

The area gets its name from the meatpacking facility that used to be located on the island in the late 1880s. The abundance of salt in the Laguna Madre made it the perfect place to pack up meats and ship them north along the coast. Salt was one of the few ways meat could be shipped or stored for any length of time before the advent of refrigeration. I imagine the area smelled awful on a steamy hot day.

The Oak Motte Sanctuary is just a block from Sand Dollar Avenue. It also features a nice boardwalk, pavilion, water features, and of course some of the most cared-for coastal oaks in Texas.

Just past the oak motte along the bay is a second parking lot that is popular with anglers and kayakers; it is also a great spot to pull up and bird from the car in the fall and winter. The channel that flows between the Laguna Madre and Gulf of Mexico is full of fish and fish eaters: American White and Brown Pelicans, Tricolored Herons, Reddish Egrets, American Oystercatchers, Herring Gulls, and Caspian and Royal Terns all gather on the spits and shore. There are also likely to be Ruddy Turnstones scampering about, flipping over stones in search of a tasty meal.

If you drive across Highway 361 toward Port Aransas, there is a parking lot on the Gulf side of the channel that is also a good birding location. Parking lot birding can take many forms. I've pulled into the parking lot on more than one occasion to take a phone call or send an email while in the area for work. On my last visit, I spotted seventeen species of birds while on a conference call.

⋙ Feather Fact ⋘

Brown Pelican: I refer to majestic Brown Pelicans as the "come-back kids." These iconic coastal birds almost became extinct by the 1960s. The insecticide DDT weakened the shells of their eggs, which made them susceptible to cracking. Brown Pelicans incubate their eggs with their feet, so weak eggs were devastating for the population. Delisted from US Fish and Wildlife's endangered species list in 1985 and from the threatened list in 2009, the populations are considered stable, the result of hard-fought conservation efforts. Squadrons can often be seen flying in formation along the surf and beaches. When they spot a fish, they plunge into the water to snatch it up for a meal. They can live more than forty years but are still vulnerable to the harsh effects of oil and chemical spills along the coasts.

FIGURE 7.8. A squadron of Brown Pelicans (photo by Jennifer L. Bristol).

FIGURE 7.9. Brown Pelican catching a fish (photo by Jennifer l. Bristol).

FIGURE 7.10. Brown Pelican eating a fish (photo by Jennifer L. Bristol).

Port Aransas Nature Preserve at Charlie's Pasture (287 species)
Port Street, Port Aransas, TX 78373
https://www.cityofportaransas.org/Nature_Preserve.cfm
Parking Lots, Short Trails, Boardwalks, Observation Platform

I love Port A: I love the beaches, the birding, the small-town feel, and the seafood, especially at Shells Pasta & Seafood. Coming across on the ferry takes me back to my childhood when we would visit my parents' friends during the summer. As an adult, I appreciate it for some of the best birding in the country, but when I was a kid, we rarely saw Brown Pelicans.

The City of Port Aransas has invested heavily in improving Charlie's Pasture and other city parks to make them accessible to people with all abilities. It's easy to mill around the various wetlands and prairies on the wide, durable surface paths and boardwalks. I recommend starting at the pavilion by the ponds and wandering along the paths for as long as you are able.

The ponds are birding bonanzas. The pavilion looks out over wetlands filled with ducks, shorebirds, swallows, and passing hawks. During April and May Black-necked Stilts, Dunlins, Least and Western Sandpipers, Willets, and Greater Yellowlegs can all be found wading and feeding in the shallow waters. The wetlands are also occupied with larger colonial nesting birds such as Great Blue and Tricolored Herons; Great, Snowy and Reddish Egrets; and Roseate Spoonbills.

I've spotted a Groove-billed Ani in the bushes next to the parking lot on more than one occasion. At first I thought I was seeing an oversized grackle until I heard its pretty voice and realized it was something different. I have seen plenty of Logger-headed Shrikes here as well and often thought they were Northern Mockingbirds at first glance.

As the saying goes, birds of a feather flock together. Keep that in mind when birding this location, as the slightest change in vegetation or depth of water invites new birds. One of the coolest birds I've ever seen from the boardwalk is the Horned Lark, which is about the size of a large sparrow. You will know it when you see it, as it is the only bird with black tufts of feathers that look like horns atop its yellow-and-black head.

The grasslands can be a jackpot for sparrows, Crested Caracaras, Northern Harriers, Scissor-tailed Flycatchers, and Dickcissels. During spring and fall, Ruby-throated and Black-chinned Hummingbirds race about looking for nectar from the native plants. In fact, the area hosts a hummingbird festival every fall to celebrate the tenacious little birds. Fall and winter also bring in large flocks of Redheads, Blue-winged and Green-winged Teals, and even Common Loons. It is worth the time to check out the ship channel to look for Magnificent Frigatebirds or dolphins following the fishing boats and tankers as they sail past.

The parking lot has a self-composting pit bathroom that is clean, but other than that, there is not yet a restroom or nature center at this location. This park was hit hard during Hurricane Harvey in August 2017. The City of Port Aransas started rebuilding and improving the preserve during 2018 and has a master plan to connect the surrounding parks with walking trails.

>>> **Feather Fact** <<<

Reddish Egret: This is a really comical bird. Reddish Egrets often arch their wings above their heads like a cape and then dash about in a frenzy as they hunt for fish or frogs. Their reddish color and pink bill with a dark tip set them apart from other egrets. They are also enjoyable to see because their populations are still declining, which makes it feel special to observe one. According to Texas Parks and Wildlife Department there are only fifteen hundred to two thousand nesting pairs in the United States. A group of egrets has many amusing names, including skewer, wedge, congregation, and RSVP.

FIGURE 7.11. Reddish Egret hunting (photo by Thomas Nilles).

Leonabelle Turnball Birding Center (326 species)
1356 Ross Avenue, Port Aransas, TX 78373
https://www.cityofportaransas.org/leonabelle_turnbull_birding_center.cfm
Parking Lot, Wastewater Treatment Facility, Boardwalk

Drive around the corner from the nearby birding location at the Joan and Scott Holt Paradise Pond to the wastewater treatment plant and get ready for a birding jackpot during the spring migration. The yard and trees located past the parking lot are typically filled with hungry warblers, orioles, vireos, and flycatchers during the spring. The birders can get as thick as the birds themselves, and sometimes they can even be a little annoying in their ambition to get the "perfect" photo of a rare passerine.

The boardwalk and pavilion that were rebuilt after Hurricane Harvey offer a good vantage point to view the marsh. From the raised platform it is easy to spot Soras, Least Bitterns, Pied-billed Grebes, Ruddy Ducks, Neotropic Cormorants, and American Coots. American Bitterns also live among the reeds but are elusive and hard to spot unless they literally walk up onto the deck, as one did while I was birding the area one fall. Keep an eye to the sky for passing Roseate Spoonbills, American Avocets, Caspian and Common Terns, and Ospreys. On more than one occasion, I have seen Belted Kingfishers sitting on the utility poles and wires that run along the road. There are two resident alligators that prowl around the marshes keeping the nutria in check and are good incentive to stay on the designated path.

This location is symbolic of why habitat matters. This small remnant of the coastal estuaries, prairies, and trees is a reminder of what the barrier island would have looked like before the relentless march of development. This location and the Joan and Scott Holt Paradise Pond are also great examples of what a few caring citizens can do to trigger a conservation movement in a community. Protecting bird habitats has resulted in millions of dollars being infused into the local economy every year because the number of birders has increased. Note that there is not a restroom at this birding center.

American Bittern: It is easier to hear this marsh-dwelling bird than to see it. When American Bitterns feel threatened, they stand perfectly still with their beaks thrust skyward. Their streaky brown-and-gray plumage offers additional camouflage that helps them blend into the reeds of a wetland. They are stealthy carnivores that will eat everything from frogs to fish to moths. They winter in Texas and along the Gulf of Mexico and return to their breeding ground in the northern parts of North America during the summer. They are mostly solitary except during migration and breeding.

FIGURE 7.12. American Bittern (photo by Jennifer L. Bristol).

FIGURE 7.13. American Bittern standing like a reed (photo by Jennifer L. Bristol).

Connie Hagar Cottage Sanctuary (215 species)
1401 South Church Street, Rockport, TX 78382
http://aransaspathways.com/connie-hagar-cottage-sanctuary/
Parking Lot, Short Trail, Observation Platform

There isn't much to the Connie Hagar Cottage Sanctuary; however, the City of Rockport is investing in some improvements. The small 6.5-acre sanctuary of live oak trees fills with migrant birds in the spring, and the observation platform is a good vantage point to look for hawks during the fall and to peer into the treetops. In 2019 a new education pavilion was added along with a pollinator garden and improved walking trails. Watch for Eastern Wood-Pewees, Eastern Phoebes, Couch's Kingbirds, and Northern Mockingbirds to launch from the branches after a bug or to claim their territory. During the spring watch for Hooded Warblers, Common Yellow Warblers, Northern Parulas, and White-eyed Vireos.

Most important, it is good to stop and pay homage to the "First Lady of Texas Birding." Connie Hagar and her husband lived in Rockport where they ran the Rockport Cottages starting in 1935. She observed the birds daily and blew the snobby eastern ornithologists' minds when she claimed to have figured out the migration patterns of many birds. After all, what could a little lady from Texas know about birds or anything else for that matter? For over thirty years she documented every bird: its behavior, plumage, food preferences, and what time of day it arrived on the Texas coast during the spring migration.

"I don't feel that I know a bird until I know it in any plumage and the way it acts," Hagar said. "I cannot understand how some people are satisfied to have a bird pointed out to them, then just put it down on a list and go away without studying it."

In 1937 her articles caught the eye of famed biologist Harry Oberholser, who was writing a book about Texas birds. He was skeptical of her accounts and in August of that year paid her a visit, questioning her methods and findings over the course of several days. At the end of his time with Connie he acknowledged she was the real deal and her findings were as reliable as any by a formally trained biologist.

Connie actively recorded the bird activity of Aransas County and the surrounding area until she was well into her eighties. For many of those years she was joined by her sister, who shared Connie's love of nature. Because of Connie's reports and articles in local papers, Rockport has been a hotspot for birders since the 1930s.

Yellow Warbler: Listen for a tweeting song that says *sweet sweet I'm so sweet*, the signature sound of this brightly colored warbler. Yellow Warblers eat mostly worms and insects, so they aren't frequent visitors at feeders; however, they will visit drips and watering stations to take a quick bath. Few creatures look as joyful as a Yellow Warbler taking a bath after a long journey during migration. Both males and females are bright yellow, but the males have a more rusty-streaked chest. They winter in Central and South America and breed in North America where willows and wet thickets occur.

FIGURE 7.14. Male Yellow Warbler just arriving in Texas during the spring migration (photo by Jennifer L. Bristol).

FIGURE 7.15. Yellow Warbler taking a bath (photo by Jennifer L. Bristol).

Rockport Beach Park (238 species)
319 Broadway Street, Rockport, TX 78382
http://www.rockportbeach-texas.com
Parking Lot

This park seems to be little more than a spit of land along the beach. But it is so much more. The park along Little Bay in Rockport is the breeding and nesting site for more than twenty species of birds, including Black Skimmers and Laughing Gulls.

The island in the middle of Little Bay serves as a rookery for Great Blue Herons, Roseate Spoonbills, and egrets. Of the birds that nest around the bay each year, over half are in decline; loss of habitat and food sources are to blame. Nonetheless, this park offers the flocks a safe haven and makes it easy to enjoy the birds year-round.

For a long time I resisted coming to the location because I thought it was nothing more than a city park that would be filled with tourists. How wrong I was. I'm sure during the summer it gets busy, but during the spring and fall it is a birding paradise. I took some of my best photos of shorebirds during the magic hours of sunset at this park.

After I realized the value of the location, it is now always a stop on our birding trips and competitions. One of the things I love most about the park is that you really start to understand the term "birds of a feather flock together." The nesting skimmers, gulls, and terns each claim a piece of the grassy lawn to nest and rear their young. It's also a cool place to sit and watch Snow Geese and Sandhill Cranes fly over during February and March. It is easy to see more than twenty species of birds at the park on any given day regardless of the season.

Rockport in general is a great place to bird year-round. The City of Rockport in collaboration with a number of other organizations hosts the Hummingbird Celebration during September and Whooping Crane Festival in February.

Black Skimmer: This bird is the only one in North America whose lower beak (mandible) is longer than the top one. A black hood masks its eyes, giving it a mysterious look. Black Skimmers fly low over the water to skim up shrimp and fish; when the beak senses prey, it snaps shut. Skimming the water to feed makes them susceptible to the ill effects of chemical or oil spills that rest on the surface of the water. Highly social, these birds are most often seen in groups called a scoop or embezzlement. Like many shorebirds, they depend on beaches for places to nest. Development and increased beach activity from humans along coastal regions have impacted the success of their breeding rate.

FIGURE 7.16. Black Skimmers on the beach in Rockport (photo by Jennifer L. Bristol).

Goose Island State Park (349 species)
202 South Palmetto Street, Rockport, TX 78382
https://tpwd.texas.gov/state-parks/goose-island
Parking Lot, Campground, Short Walk, Bird Blind

Goose Island State Park is home to the second-largest live oak tree in the state of Texas; the largest is at the San Bernard National Wildlife Refuge. Unlike much of the region, the park is set in a live oak forest that juts out into the bay. It is worth it to pay a visit to the thousand-year-old tree and its surrounding offspring; just standing in the tree's presence is a humbling experience. It is also worth the time to observe the birds that frequent the property across the street from the big tree or down by the bay. On more than one occasion I have seen Sandhill and Whooping Cranes in this area.

The live oak trees and shallow bays are a haven for migrating birds coming from South America on their long journey across the Gulf of Mexico. Nature's perfectly timed dance fills the trees with caterpillars and other emerging bugs that act as a proverbial buffet for the long-distance travelers.

The park has set up two small drips with a birdbath, brush pile, and feeders in the campground that are maintained by volunteers and staff. The feeding station near the restroom is a great place to hang out in the shade of the trees during the morning or afternoon on a warm spring day in April to watch for arriving warblers and resident birds. With luck, the migrating birds will drop in around 4:00 p.m. or are still lingering in the morning.

Why 4:00 p.m.? Well, that's what Connie Hagar figured out. The birds make their leap of faith from Yucatán the night before and fly all night and day across the Gulf of Mexico to arrive on the Texas coast in late afternoon. As they arrive, the trees will fill with Baltimore Orioles; Indigo Buntings; Common Yellowthroat; and Cerulean, Blue-winged, Nashville, and dozens of other warblers. Partners in Flight reports that the Cerulean Warbler has suffered a 72 percent drop in population between 1970 and 2014, making it one of the warblers of highest concern. Conservation of breeding habitat in North America is critical for the survival of the Cerulean and other warblers.

It is also worth your time to go out to the shoreline of the bay. I recommend strolling through the campground and out to the observation deck to look for Ruddy Turnstones, Great Egrets, American White Pelicans, Tricolored and Little Blue Herons, and Black-necked Stilts. During the winter months it is easy to see flocks of Canada Geese, Sandhill Cranes, Northern Shovelers, and Northern Pintails drifting through the sky. If you are lucky, you might catch a glimpse of endangered Whooping Cranes flying overhead or feeding in the restored wetlands.

I recommend camping in the park during the fall and winter before the bugs are too thick. If you camp during the spring or summer, be sure to bring your bug spray and check the mosquito netting on your tent for holes.

≫ **Feather Fact** ≪

Piping Plover: This tiny sandy-colored bird with a broken dark collar around its neck is fun to watch scampering about on the beaches of the Gulf of Mexico and Atlantic. Piping Plovers are also enjoyable to see because they are considered an endangered species. The population that lives along the Atlantic is more stable than those that migrate to the Great Lakes and upper parts of the Great Plains. The Great Lakes population was down to just a few dozen nesting pairs in the mid-1980s. Loss of habitat and disturbance to nesting sites are listed as major reasons for the drop in populations. Because they are frightened easily, they will leave their nests to try to draw away predators or move out of the way of humans. When they do so, they leave the eggs or chicks open to predation from just about anything that enjoys eating eggs.

FIGURE 7.17. Piping Plovers (photo by Jennifer L. Bristol).

Aransas National Wildlife Refuge (368 species)
1 Wild Life Circle, Austwell, TX 77950
https://www.fws.gov/refuge/aransas/
Parking Lots, Short Trails, Observation Platform, Driving Tour

The lush 153,000-acre Aransas National Wildlife Refuge borders San Antonio Bay and is the winter home of the endangered Whooping Cranes. By 1941 the Whoopers were down to just 15 birds in the wild, but through conservation efforts in the United States and Canada the birds have made a slow comeback to around 420 cranes in the wild.

The refuge is also home to more than 350 species of birds and other important coastal wildlife, including the Kemp's ridley sea turtle. It isn't always easy to see the Whooping Cranes when they are at the refuge from October to March. I have taken a lot of pictures of a decoy that I was convinced was just a very cooperative crane. The best way to see the Whoopers is to take one of the private tours offered out of Rockport or kayak along San Antonio Bay. On occasion the birds can be seen flying across Saint Charles Bay toward Goose Island State Park.

The driving tour takes visitors on a nice journey to each of the bird blinds, short walks, and observation decks. Some of the structures were damaged in Hurricane Harvey but are on track to be rebuilt. Despite the loss of the structures, the birds still hang out in the marshes, fields, and large oak mottes.

During February when the Whoopers are in the area, the park is also home to Surf Scoters, Lesser Scaups, Snow Geese, Northern Pintails, Ring-necked Ducks, Black-bellied Plovers, and Long-billed Curlews. During the spring migration shores, trees, fields, and skies light up with every sort of migrant. I have had the best luck seeing the migrant songbirds in the trees around the visitor center.

The refuge is a little off the beaten path, so I recommend packing a lunch and a lot of water to make a day of it. The refuge is good for birding pretty much year-round, so whatever day you decide to visit, make sure you give yourself plenty of time to stop at several (or all) of the points along the way, especially the tower at Live Oak Point and the visitor center.

Whooping Crane: This crane is the largest bird in North America and one of the most endangered. During the 1940s the magnificent Whooping Crane had a population of only 15 in the wild. Through strategic conservation efforts there are now around 600 birds (only 420 in the wild). Protected under the Migratory Bird Treaty Act and the Endangered Species Act, each one is banded and carefully monitored. Whooping Cranes mate for life and live more than twenty years. They travel from Texas to Canada's Wood Buffalo National Park, where they nest and fledge their young. San Antonio Bay is famous for blue crab, which is a preferred meal for the Whoopers.

FIGURE 7.18. Whooping Crane (photo by Thomas Nilles).

FIGURE 7.19. Whooping Cranes on the wing (photo by Jennifer L. Bristol)

8 · Rio Grande Valley

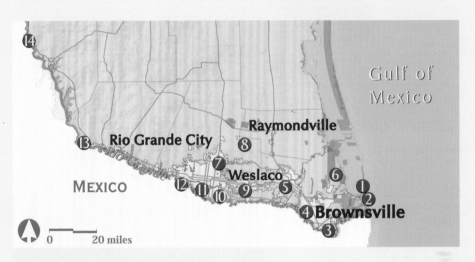

RIO GRANDE VALLEY REGION
KEY:

1   South Padre Island Birding Center (SPIBC) and Convention Center
2   Sheepshead Valley Land Trust Lots
3   Sabal Palm Audubon Sanctuary
4   Resaca de la Palma State Park
5   Hugh Ramsey Nature Park
6   Laguna Atascosa Wildlife Refuge
7   Edinburg Scenic Wetlands
8   Delta Lake Park
9   Estero Llano Grande State Park
10 Santa Ana National Wildlife Refuge
11 Quinta Mazatlan
12 Bentsen–Rio Grande Valley State Park
13 Roma Bluffs
14 San Ygnacio Bird Sanctuary

FIGURE 8.1. Clapper Rail (photo by Jennifer L. Bristol).

FIGURE 8.2. Olive Sparrow (photo by Jennifer L. Bristol).

FIGURE 8.3. Warbling Vireo (photo by Jennifer L. Bristol).

FIGURE 8.4. Couch's Kingbird (photo by Jennifer L. Bristol).

If you are looking for a grand valley in this area, you won't find one. The Rio Grande Valley is better defined as the South Texas Brush Country, which consists of thorny plants, stinging bugs, and rattling snakes. The subtropical region is also known as one of the major agricultural producers in the country where groves of oranges mix with fields of onions, lettuce, sugar cane, and of course corn. Most important, it is one of the best places to bird in the world, and there are nine World Birding Centers in the region.

Along the *resacas*, or remnants of the Rio Grande, small forests of hackberry, mesquite, palm, and ebony exist as havens for wildlife and birds alike. There are many species of birds that can be seen only in the Valley in the United States. The warm winters also attract thousands of North American snowbirds, otherwise known as Minnesotans, Canadians, Ohioans, and other northerners trying to escape the harsh winters of their homeland for a little fun in the sun. Because of the mild winters and booming economy the region now has the eighth-largest population in the United States. The rapid growth has put stress on the habitats and wildlife of the area that support the large nature tourism economy. Thankfully there is a strong network of organizations working to conserve as much of the habitats as they can before they are turned into yet another shopping center or housing development.

The area has miles of coastline along the Gulf of Mexico and the Lower Laguna Madre. The Laguna Madre is a massive expanse of shallow, brackish water rimmed with marshes and thornscrub that attracts a range of graceful shorebirds, gulls, terns, and migrants.

South Padre Island Birding Center (SPIBC) (341 species) and Convention Center (356 species)
6801 Padre Boulevard, South Padre Island, TX 78597
https://www.spibirding.com
Parking Lots, Nature Center Campus, Boardwalks

If I were going to get someone interested in birding, I would take them to these two locations. The birding from the SPIBC or the Convention Center grounds is excellent year-round. These two sites are located next to each other, but they are not connected. They share the same birds, wetlands, and airspace but are completely separate properties. It might feel as though you could jump across the chasm to the parallel boardwalk, but I don't recommend risking it with the hungry alligators lurking in the reeds below. However, it is worth visiting both areas. I enjoy the quaint gift shop and the staff at SPIBC and always make a point to visit. The SPIBC also offers guided bird walks that are worth taking to really learn about the South Texas coastal birds.

Herons, rails, gulls, ducks, and other shorebirds fill the wetlands, while Ospreys and Peregrine Falcons hunt high overhead. During the spring migration the trees and reeds at both locations are filled with more than thirty-five species of warblers and seven types of vireos in addition to brilliantly colored birds such as Baltimore Orioles, Scarlet Tanagers, Ruby-throated Hummingbirds, Indigo Buntings, and Rose-breasted Grosbeaks. While strolling along the boardwalk at any time of year, it is common to find Black-bellied Whistling Ducks, Red-winged Blackbirds, Common and Purple Gallinules, Great Blue Herons, and Soras feeding or resting in the shallow marshes.

Our birding team started one of our Great Texas Birding Classic six-day events here and counted more than one hundred species of birds before we left the island at noon. Unlike most places, dawn birding is not ideal at this location. Unless you are willing to settle for the lousy coffee at the motel or from a gas station, you can't get a cup of the good stuff before 8:00 a.m. Be ready to slow your roll and embrace island time; the birds wake up slowly as well.

I believe that during the spring migration, the best time to be on the island ready to bird is in the late afternoon. The birds start arriving to the island around mid- to late afternoon from their long flight across the coast. If the winds are right, they will drop down on the barrier islands in search of fresh water and food. If the winds are strong out of the south, the birds might fly over the island and land in the Tamaulipan thorn-scrub of the mainland, which means it might be best to head inland to the Laguna Atascosa Wildlife Refuge. The weather plays a big factor in what you might see from season to season or even day to day during the migration.

Our birding team has been on the island for a fallout, and it is a life experience none of us will forget. The birds were landing in the parking lots, on the beaches, in the trees, on any solid thing they could find. Volunteers were putting out fruit and fresh water all around the island to help the avian friends recover from a long and difficult flight. I took some of my best photos of warblers during that time. They were exhausted and moving slowly, so I could actually capture their beauty with my camera. But they don't stay long. Once the winds changed and the birds are fueled up, they take to the wing at night and make their way north along ancient flyways to their nesting habitats.

⋙ Feather Fact ⋘

Common Gallinule: If you hear a sound like someone who has just sucked the air out of a helium balloon and is laughing hysterically off in the reeds, that's the Common Gallinule. These sleek black rails have a distinctive red shield over their bills. Their unusual large yellow-green feet are adapted to walking across mudflats or floating material. They are good swimmers despite not having webbed feet and can often be seen in groups with American Coots. They are short-distance migrants that fly at night; however, a large population can be found year-round in South Texas.

FIGURE 8.5. Purple Gallinule (photo by Jennifer L. Bristol).

Sheepshead Valley Land Trust Lots (279 species)
111 West Sheepshead Street, South Padre Island, TX 78597
https://valleylandfund.com/conservation-efforts/
Parking Lot

This tiny birding location consists of two lots managed by the Valley Land Trust. This small spot of habitat has four drips and several large trees that are enticing to the migrating birds. During the spring migration, birds fill the trees around the drips and feed off fruit left out by volunteers. I've spotted Canada, Kentucky, Blackburnian, and Hooded Warblers here along with Baltimore and Orchard Orioles. Check the ground around the drips for Ovenbirds, Gray-cheeked and Wood Thrushes, and Gray Catbirds. The warblers that pass through the island are too numerous to list; however, the joyful-looking Common Yellowthroat can be found at this location and others on the island year-round.

There is a chalkboard where visitors record what they are seeing each day that is worth a look to get an idea of what is in the area. This is another great example of what a few concerned citizens can achieve when they collaborate to conserve habitat for wildlife. There is no restroom at this location; however, it is very close to the main street of the island where the majority of the businesses are located.

⁑ Feather Fact ⁘

Black-throated Green Warbler: One of the first warblers to arrive in Texas during the spring migration, this distinctive yellow, black, and white bird is a showstopper. And the males do so love to put on a show. Once they reach the breeding grounds in the boreal forests of North America, they will sing with an undying spirit. It is easier to see them during the migration, as once they are in the north, they move continuously through the midrange of the thick tree canopy. These long-distance migrants prefer to fly overland during the migration and will reach Texas around the end of March. Despite habitat loss and fragmentation, their populations are stable and have even slightly increased.

FIGURE 8.6. Male Black-throated Green Warbler (photo by Jennifer L. Bristol).

Sabal Palm Audubon Sanctuary (337 species)
8435 Sabal Palm Grove Road, Brownsville, TX 78521
http://sabalpalmsanctuary.org
Parking Lot, Nature Center Campus, Short Walk, Observation Platform

Get ready for an adventure when visiting this location. This is about as far south as you can go to bird and still be in the United States. To get there, you have to slip behind the border fence, which makes the journey seem like something from a spy novel. In reality, the birding center is welcoming and safe. The 527-acre sanctuary was forced to close in 2009 when the section of border fence was built but reopened in 2011, and visitors could again explore the palm forest, which is just one of two remaining stands left in the region.

Built in 1892, the Rabb family plantation house has been converted into a nature center where guests can bird the gardens close to the house or stroll along the thick tropical forest to one of the ponds. Sometimes there is a Great Horned Owl that nests in the sabal palms close to the house; just ask the volunteers to point it out. I typically check the bird list posted in the visitor center before wandering off on one of the trails. I also recommend signing up for one of the guided nature walks to learn from the experienced staff and volunteers.

There is a trail that leads over to the Rio Grande, where you will have the best chance for seeing a Ringed, Belted, or Green Kingfisher. At the small lake located off the Resaca Loop Trail I've spotted Least, Pied-billed, and Eared Grebes in addition to Black-crowned and Yellow-crowned Night-Herons, Anhingas, and a number of shore-birds. It's best to get a map at the visitor center before heading out on the trails, as the forest is intensely thick and can be a little disorienting. I don't rely on my cell phone at this location because it usually switches over to the Mexican cell service and charges extra fees.

Black-crowned Night-Heron: This small, stocky bird is the most widely distributed of all the herons. These herons are highly social, and adults do not distinguish between chicks within they large roosts. Juveniles have a brownish body with yellowish eyes that turn a deep red when the birds become mature adults. They will live in tidal pools, lakes, ponds, marshes, or just about any body of water that supplies the terrestrial and aquatic foods they prefer. True to their name, they prefer to hunt at night to avoid competition. I have frequently seen them in the evening along the Riverwalk in San Antonio.

FIGURE 8.7. Black-crowned Night-Heron (photo by Jennifer L. Bristol).

Resaca de la Palma State Park (294 species)

1000 New Carmen Avenue, Brownsville, TX 78521
https://tpwd.texas.gov/state-parks/resaca-de-la-palma
Parking Lots, Short Trails, Bird Blinds, Observation Platform, Tram Tour

At times the Rio Grande Valley can feel overfilled with people and the trappings of a rapidly growing metro area. This state park is a welcome retreat with twelve hundred acres of semitropical wilderness to explore.

Because the park is so large, it offers a tram tour to transport visitors to the various decks and bird blinds to search for Grasshopper and Lark Sparrows, Blue Grosbeaks, or Wild Turkeys. The mix of wetlands, grasslands, thornscrub, and forests makes the park attractive to resident Valley birds and passerines alike. When I think of this park, I think about birds of color. Altamira, Bullock's, Hooded, and Orchard Orioles all frequent the area in April and May. Great Kiskadees and Green Jays mix it up with visiting warblers during the migrations, while the wetlands fill with a variety of shorebirds when there is water to support them. In April alone more than 210 species have been spotted at the park.

If you don't have time for the tram tour, you can see plenty of species at the parking area, bird blinds, and feeding stations around the visitor center. The park is open Wednesday to Sunday, so don't show up at 7:00 a.m. on a Monday expecting to bird anything more than the parking area near the front gate.

> ### ⫸ Feather Fact ⫷
>
> **Altamira Oriole:** This orange-and-black bird is native to Mexico and can be found only in the Rio Grande Valley in the United States. The males and females share the same markings and are commonly seen together once they have partnered up for the season. They build fibrous nests out of moss and other materials that hang from trees or power lines. They prefer to dine on insects, spiders, fruits, and berries, and since the citrus industry is alive and well in the Rio Grande Valley, they have ample food in the region.
>
>
>
> FIGURE 8.8. Altamira Oriole (photo by Jennifer L. Bristol).

Hugh Ramsey Nature Park (269 species)
706 East Taft Avenue, Harlingen, TX 78550
http://www.theworldbirdingcenter.com/harlingen.html
Parking Lot, Short Trail, Bird Blinds

Whatever you do, don't wander off into the wilderness at this place on a hundred-degree day. Stick to the bird blinds that are a few yards from the parking lot. Hugh Ramsey Park connects with the Harlingen Thicket to create a nice-sized chunk of habitat, but it is easy to get lost if you are unfamiliar with the trails.

This park is part of the World Birding Center network and quickly won my favor during my first visit. There are two excellent bird blinds close to the parking lot. Both have water features and are nestled among the ebony forest and thornscrub. Even on a hot, windy day in the spring, the birds were abundant. Kentucky, Chestnut-sided, Bay-breasted, Mourning, and Yellow Warblers all pass through in the spring alongside the brightly colored Hooded Orioles. Our team did not make it to the blind north of the parking area, although it looks promising because it is located near a pond. Resident birds include; Harris's Hawks, Plain Chachchalacas, White-tipped Doves, Bewick's Wrens, and Buff-bellied Hummingbirds.

My family were real troupers on this adventure. In the heat, coupled with a total lack of knowledge of the park and the trails, our outing could have taken a turn for the worse. However, the birding was so good that we rallied together to score several life-list species, including the Green Kingfisher, who perched on a dead tree just above the green waters of the creek.

While bumbling down the trails in the scorching heat, I spotted a piece of paper lying on the ground. It was a letter from a teacher to a student, although it was hard to determine if it was a high school or college student. The teacher was offering a pep talk to the student to stay in school and reach his full potential. The letter captured our imagination and sent us off into a thousand splintered thoughts of speculation and wonder. I was grateful for the entertainment the letter provided, as it gave me time to find the right trail and get the team back to the shade of the bird blinds. You never know what you might discover while out exploring in nature.

Plain Chachalaca: This chicken-sized bird can be found from the Rio Grande Valley into Central America. I love the description by the Cornell Lab of Ornithology that the bird has the "grace of a bulldozer." Indeed, Plain Chachalacas are not graceful, but they are amazingly tender and affectionate to each other once they have paired up. You will most likely hear them before you see them, as they issue brash calls to each other starting early in the morning. It is common to find them in large groups patrolling the feeding stations of certain parks or around fruit-bearing trees.

FIGURE 8.9. Male Plain Chachalaca in courtship (photo by Jennifer L. Bristol).

Laguna Atascosa Wildlife Refuge (359 species)

22688 Buena Vista Boulevard, Los Fresnos, TX 78566
https://www.fws.gov/refuge/laguna_atascosa/
Parking Lots, Nature Center Campus, Short Trails, Driving Tour

This national wildlife refuge is best known for protecting the endangered ocelot; however, the thousands of acres of habitat are also home to hundreds of species of birds. The drive to get to the refuge is long but worth it. Around the visitor center there are several feeding and water stations where Green Jays and White-tipped Doves congregate. The short Kiskadee Trail meanders around the visitor center where more than three hundred species of birds have been recorded. In April more than fifteen species of warblers and five types of vireos pass through, while Yellow-billed Cuckoos, Buff-bellied Hummingbirds, Common Nighthawks, and Brown-crested Flycatchers arrive in April and stay until September. While enjoying the grounds of the visitor center and the short trail or the parking area, keep an eye on the sky to watch for gulls, terns, hawks, or geese flying by as they move from the inland lakes and fields out to Laguna Madre.

If the driving tour along Bayside Drive is open, take the time to see if you can spot endangered Aplomado Falcons. These steel-gray falcons were listed as endangered in 1986 and reintroduced in the 1990s, with the Laguna Atascosa National Wildlife Refuge being the center for the new population.

From November to March the ducks and shorebirds are abundant around the lake along with raptors such as White-tailed Kites, Cooper's Hawks, Northern Harriers, and White-tailed Hawks. The large chestnut, gray, and white Harris's Hawk can be found in the region year-round and can often be seen hunting in pairs across the refuge.

I recommend visiting in the morning or evening when the temperature is a little more forgiving. The refuge offers bird walks and other educational programs when there is funding for staff or enough qualified volunteers. This refuge and all other national wildlife refuges often have their budgets cut and rely heavily on volunteers to run their programs. If you plan on walking in this park, take plenty of water and a map and know your limits.

Wilson's Warbler: This bright flash of yellow can be found wintering in the Rio Grande Valley and into Central America. Once these warblers start to migrate, they fan out across all lower forty-eight states to reach their breeding habitats in the mountainous regions of Oregon, Washington, Montana, and northern Canada. Males sport a jaunty black cap, while females are all yellow, much like the Yellow Warblers, but slightly smaller. Despite the size of the breeding range their populations are in steep decline due to habitat loss and the parasitic habits of the Brown-headed Cowbird. They are one of the smallest warblers and never seem to stop moving as they feed along shrubs and the lower parts of trees.

FIGURE 8.10. Wilson's Warbler (photo by Thomas Nilles).

Edinburg Scenic Wetlands (293 species)

714 Raul Longoria, Edinburg, TX 78542
http://www.edinburgwbc.org
Parking Lot, Nature Center Campus, Short Trails

The Edinburg World Birding Center is a city park run by one of the most knowledge-able and friendly teams in the Valley. If you have the time, sign up for one of the guided birding walks or classes. Or you can just stroll along the well-maintained grounds and short trails around the nature center to discover why this location is a must when visiting the Valley.

The center is located on forty acres of thornscrub and wetlands, which draw in more than twelve species of ducks and a variety of shorebirds in addition to Valley specialties such as Great Kiskadees, Green Jays, Buff-bellied Hummingbirds, Green Kingfishers, Couch's Kingbirds, and Fulvous Whistling-Ducks. On more than one occasion a Long-Eared Owl has been photographed near the visitor center. As always, it is important to remember that there is no guarantee of what birds you might see on any given day, so it is always fun to return to find new species to add to your list.

> ### ⋙ Feather Fact ⋘
>
> **Spotted Sandpiper:** Look along the water's edge for a spotted shorebird that teeters when it walks, which is how you will identify the Spotted Sandpiper. During the breeding season, a female mates with multiple males and leaves her partners with the nesting duties while she defends the territory. While in Texas during the winter, Spotted Sandpipers are most commonly seen alone. A group of sandpipers is known as a fling, hill, or time-step. Who comes up with these names?

FIGURE 8.11. Spotted Sandpiper (photo by Jennifer L. Bristol).

Delta Lake Park (259 species)
28051 North FM 88, Monte Alto, TX 78538
https://www.hidalgocounty.us/394/Delta-Lake-Park
Parking Lots, Short Trail

The birding here is good year-round, but it gets particularly exciting during the winter months when the ducks, geese, shorebirds, and hawks show up. This is a well-used community park with lots of parking and plenty of places to have a picnic. I recommend putting the picnic tables to use and spending a few hours milling around the fields and trail along the lake.

Mottled, Ruddy, and Ring-necked Ducks; Redheads; and Northern Pintails mix with Least and Pied-billed Grebes and Snow and Greater White-fronted Geese during January and February. Bonaparte's, Herring, Laughing, and Ring-billed Gulls are also attracted to the large reservoir during the winter months. It is common to see and hear Sandhill Cranes pass overhead as they move from the fields to their roosts.

During April and May the Great Crested and Scissor-tailed Flycatchers arrive alongside Barn, Cave, Cliff, Northern Rough-winged, and Tree Swallows to feed on the ample collection of insects. Resident birds include Great Kiskadees, Vermilion Flycatchers, Tropical Kingbirds, and Curve-billed Thrashers. From Memorial Day to Labor Day the park can get busy with families fishing and enjoying the lake, but the birding is still decent despite the increase in human activity.

⋙ Feather Fact ⋘

Black-bellied Whistling Duck: If you see a funny-looking duck with long pink legs, pink bill, and black belly perched on a fence post, deck, or log, then you are looking at a Black-bellied Whistling Duck. Once called "Tree Ducks," these short-distance migrants can be found year-round in South Texas. They are easy to distinguish by their chattering, as they sound like they have swallowed a child's whistle and are trying to get it unstuck from their long, graceful necks. Look for these ducks along wetlands of South Texas, suburban yards, golf courses, and agricultural fields where they feed, mostly at night, on vegetation and grains.

FIGURE 8.12. Black-bellied Whistling Ducks (photo by Jennifer L. Bristol).

Estero Llano Grande State Park (345 species)
3301 South International Boulevard (FM 1015), Weslaco, TX 78596
https://tpwd.texas.gov/state-parks/estero-llano-grande
Parking Lot, Nature Center Campus, Short Trails

A portion of this 230-acre birding site is a former RV park, which means it has plenty of old parking lots to explore. Visitors can walk along the old road and former campsites nestled among the large oaks, ebony, and hackberry trees to find Altamira Orioles and Northern Beardless-Tyrannulets nesting in the woods, along with Golden-fronted Woodpeckers and Olive Sparrows. If you look on eBird, there is a separate list designated for this part of the park because the habitat is different from that in the rest of the park.

The splendor of this location is the deck at the visitor center that looks out over the shallow lake of the Arroyo Colorado. My mom, who is particularly fond of the park, has often imparted her wealth of knowledge about how the park came to be, who helped create it, and why it is significant. When her knee started to cause her pain, my husband and I would station her on the deck while we walked the trails. Enviably, she would see more species while patiently watching from the deck than we spied on our hasty journey around the looping trails. The short, flat walks are worth taking if you have the time to linger and study the species and if the temperature is not scorching hot.

The deck is shaded and has easy access to the well-informed park staff and volunteers who offer excellent guided birding walks. Like most of the other World Birding Centers, there is a list of the species that have recently been identified posted near the entrance to the visitor center. The lists are helpful as they give you an idea about what you might see either in the wetlands or flying overhead. Shorebirds abound here, but keep your eyes on the skies for White-tailed Kites or Crested Caracaras.

Two night flyers nest in the park. The Common Pauraque and the Eastern Screech-Owl frequently raise their young in the Rio Grande woodlands. The Common Pauraque looks like a nighthawk when in flight and on the hunt for insects. While the Common Pauraque prefers to nest on the ground in the thornscrub, the Eastern Screech-Owl prefers to nest in tree cavities or nesting boxes.

Totally unrelated to birding, one of my family's more entrepreneurial relatives, Ed Couch, settled the towns of Weslaco and Edcouch. The family lore surmises that Ed swindled a great deal of money from the family in Haskell and made a run for the border. When he arrived in the Valley, he saw a land of opportunity and invested in starting the two towns. Actual history and family lore tell different versions of the story. The truth lies somewhere in the middle, although my grandmother, at one hundred years of age, holds fast to the family lore version; therefore, so will I.

Regardless of the truth, I'd like to have seen the wildlife and wild lands that old Ed observed in the 1920s. The Rio Grande Valley is now the eighth most-populated region in the United States, but back then it was just starting to realize its full potential as an agricultural powerhouse and would have been lightly populated by people and heavily populated with birds. Parks like Estero Llano Grande are important for our understanding of the natural history of the area and maintaining a space for our wild friends.

⫸ Feather Fact ⫷

Common Pauraque: This nightjar nests on the ground and is one of the most camouflaged species I have ever observed. The adult bird looks like a small log or rock lying among the thornscrub. It does not build a nest, which makes it even harder to spot in the underbrush. Like other ground-nesting birds, it suffers from loss of habitat to agriculture and development. These birds often fly close to the ground in an erratic pattern as they follow the bugs. The hair-like feathers around their beaks are thought to help detect insects as they fly through the night. They can be observed only in the United States in the Rio Grande Valley; however, their range extends as far south as Argentina.

FIGURE 8.13. Common Pauraque on its nest in April (photo by Jennifer L. Bristol).

FIGURE 8.14. Common Pauraque hiding in plain sight (photo by Jennifer L. Bristol).

Santa Ana National Wildlife Refuge (345 species)
3325 Green Jay Road, Alamo, TX 78516
https://www.fws.gov/refuge/santa_ana/
Parking Lot, Nature Center Campus, Short Trails, Observation Platform

The Santa Ana National Wildlife Refuge has a separate birding list for the parking area and adjacent walking trail that boasts 242 species. If you are willing to walk a little on the well-maintained walking trails, an additional 100 species can be found throughout the year in the forests and wetlands located south of the visitor center.

On our first visit in 2013, our birding team jokingly called it the "Armageddon Birding Center." The term isn't very friendly; however, the area was in a depressingly intense drought, and the once-rich ebony and hackberry forest and wetlands were dry and brittle. Where there was water, the birds flocked in droves. That trip also took us on one of our longest and least fruitful birding walks. It was great to get the exercise and explore the park, but on that day I was determined to find a jackpot of birds for our team, which we finally did at Pintail Lakes.

I've returned every year since then and find it delightfully different on every visit. I've had the best luck finding a variety of birds either around the parking area or along the Pintail Lakes Trail. The Pintail Lakes can get a little hot in the afternoon sun, so I recommend a morning or evening visit to search for Green Kingfishers, Lesser Yellow-legs, Spotted Sandpipers, Wilson's Snipes, Black-necked Stilts, or Pectoral Sandpipers. Also look out for Red-winged Blackbirds; Great-tailed Grackles; Barn, Bank, Cave, and Tree Swallows; and Black and Eastern Phoebes as they all dance around the lakes looking for insects, while Lark, Lincoln's, and Savannah Sparrows feed in the adjacent grasslands.

Four types of cuckoos exist in the park during April and May: Groove-billed Anis, Roadrunners, and Yellow-billed and Black-billed Cuckoos. Six species of doves live in the park year-round and can often be found together near the feeding stations. In the past few years a few Northern Jacanas have moved into the park during the winter months from Mexico and Central America.

The refuge offers guided birding tours that are really interesting. As at all national wildlife refuges and most nature centers, pets are not allowed at this location. The friends group runs the gift shop, which is excellent.

≫ **Feather Fact** ≪

Green Jay: The most remarkable thing about the Green Jay is its vibrant color. But Green Jays are also remarkable because they use sticks to extract insects from under a tree's bark or from a hole in a tree. They live year-round in the Rio Grande Valley, eastern Mexico, and the Yucatán. During the winter they might move slightly farther north into Texas as they look for food, but they do not migrate to breed or nest. A group of jays is called a party.

FIGURE 8.15. Green Jay (photo by Thomas Nilles).

Quinta Mazatlan (280 species)
600 Sunset Drive, McAllen, TX 78503
http://www.quintamazatlan.com
Parking Lot, Nature Center Campus, Short Trails, Bird Blinds

Take a step back in time to the grandeur of the Rio Grande Valley circa 1935. The visitor center at Quinta Mazatlan, a former luxurious home built in the Spanish Revival style, is one of the largest adobe structures in Texas, and I never get tired of wandering around its grounds.

The small pond toward the education center is a great place to see Green Herons and Belted Kingfishers hunting in the stocked pond. Buff-bellied, Ruby-throated, and Black-chinned Hummingbirds whiz by as they feed on the lovely array of flowers that bloom year-round. Occasionally, a Lucifer Hummingbird passes through and causes a stir among the birding community.

The trails that meander through the ebony and hackberry forests offer a glimpse into what the ecology would have been like prior to the agriculture boom. The large trees offer welcome shade on a warm summer, spring, or fall day and make it comfortable to spend some time observing the many birds that flock to the feeders and native plants. If you can, plan to arrive just as the center opens; you might catch sight of an Eastern Screech-Owl resting peacefully in one of the boxes mounted along the trail.

This is also one of the few places to see a Northern Beardless-Tyrannulet. Why is it beardless? I have no idea, but it is fun to think about. Baltimore, Hooded, and Orchard Orioles can all be found here from spring to fall alongside other colorful birds such as Scarlet and Summer Tanagers, Green Jays, Green Parakeets, and Red-crowned Parrots. The park recently added several acres and additional trails that are interesting to stroll around. All the trails have multiple stations where patrons can relax and watch the birds among the feeders, native plants, or water features.

⫸ **Feather Fact** ⫷

Green Heron: Unlike most herons, this greenish-brown bird has a low profile and prefers to perch above the water instead of wading through it to hunt. Green Herons are one of the few birds in North America that use a tool or bait to lure in prey. For example, they will drop bread crumbs or insects on the top of the water to lure fish to the surface. They can be found year-round along the Gulf Coast and in the summer in most parts of Texas near water. According to the North American Breeding Bird Survey this common bird is in steep decline, most likely due to habitat loss of shallow wetlands. These herons love to hunt the easy pickings of a koi fishpond or stocked fishing lake.

FIGURE 8.16. Green Heron eating a large fish (photo by Thomas Nilles).

Bentsen–Rio Grande Valley State Park (343 species)
2800 South Bentsen Palm Drive, Mission, TX 78572
https://tpwd.texas.gov/state-parks/bentsen-rio-grande-valley
Parking Lot, Nature Center Campus, Short Trails, Bird Blind, Observation Platform, Tram Tour

Bentsen–Rio Grande Valley State Park is part of the World Birding Center network that spans the region. The land was given to the State of Texas for the purpose of a park in 1944 by the parents of Senator Lloyd Bentsen. The family were prominent farmers and business leaders in the valley who also valued the natural beauty and wildlife of the region.

This park is great for people with limited mobility or young ones because there is a tram that stops at each bird blind, hawk tower, and short walking trail the park has to offer. Since the majority of the park falls behind the southern border fence, it is not possible to drive a car into the park; instead, visitors can take a tram, rent bikes, or stroll along the flat, well-maintained road. Please note that this park is one of many that shares the border with Mexico and could be altered by the addition of more border fencing.

I'm always impressed with John, the keeper of the Hawk Tower. His keen eyes can accurately spy migrating hawks that I would consider black dots on the horizon or dirt on my sunglasses. He and the other park volunteers and staff cheerfully share their birding knowledge with all new visitors and help them understand the characteristics of the passing Swainson's, Broad-winged, Gray, or Zone-tailed Hawks. The tower is wheelchair/stroller accessible; however it does get warm in the afternoon because there is not any shade at the top of the tower. It's also fun to stand on the tower and peer across the *resacas* and forest into Mexico.

The birds are attracted to the habitat, which is carefully maintained by Texas Parks and Wildlife. The rich and fertile soil deposited by the river supports forests of cedar elm, sugar hackberry, Rio Grande ash, Texas ebony, and anaqua. Each native plant supplies an important source of food with seeds, fruits, or insects. The park also maintains two feeding stations with benches where birders can relax and observe. Plain Chachalacas, Green Jays, White-tipped Doves, Inca Doves, and Golden-fronted Woodpeckers can frequently be found loitering around the feeder stations. One of my personal favorite species that spends its summers at the park is the Groove-billed Ani.

⚱ **Feather Fact** ⚱

Groove-billed Ani: This medium-sized iridescent blue-black bird is often mistaken for a grackle. But look closer at the large bill. These ancient-looking birds nest along the pasturelands and thickets of the Rio Grande Valley, where adults share a communal nest and all members of the group, or orphanage, will tend to the eggs and young. For such a brutish-looking bird, it has a high, pretty whistle. Groove-billed Anis are members of the cuckoo family and look like they just flew in from the Jurassic period.

FIGURE 8.17. Groove-billed Ani (photo by Jennifer L. Bristol).

Roma Bluffs (215 species)

612 Portscheller Street, Roma, TX 78584
http://www.theworldbirdingcenter.com/Roma.html
Parking Lot, Nature Center Campus

Roma is off the beaten path but interesting nonetheless. You won't find a big, shiny nature center here, but you will find a historic town, an interesting geological feature at the bluffs, and a good vantage point to look across the Rio Grande into Mexico.

When the birding center is open, the feeding stations bring in a variety of birds. However, the best birding takes place along the river where the Belted, Green, and Ringed Kingfishers hunt alongside Anhingas and Great Blue Herons. The area is also home to the Brown Jay and the Red-bellied Pigeon, which are not common but can be found along the river in the Rio Grande Valley. On occasion, the White-collared Seedeater stretches its northern range far enough to reach the area.

There isn't much to the town, so park in the historic district, walk down to the bluffs, pull out your optics, and start birding.

> ≫ **Feather Fact** ≪
>
> **Great Kiskadee:** If you are in the Rio Grande Valley, you are never far from the sound of this bold bird. Cornell Lab of Ornithology states that these birds "hunt like a flycatcher, fish like a kingfisher, and forage like a jay," which makes them exciting to observe. They cross into the United States only in Texas but are considered to be one of the most widely distributed flycatchers in the Americas that do not migrate. Both males and females sport a black mask, yellow body, and rust-colored wings.

FIGURE 8.18. Great Kiskadee (photo by Jennifer L. Bristol).

San Ygnacio Bird Sanctuary (264 species)
Grant Avenue and Trevino Street, San Ygnacio, TX 78067
https://tpwd.texas.gov/huntwild/wildlife/wildlife-trails/ltc/zapata-loop
Parking Lot, Bird Blind, Observation Platform

At a slight bend in the road between Laredo and Zapata is the tiny town of San Ygnacio, population seven hundred souls. Built around Uribe Plaza, the town appears to have been frozen in time after it was established around the time of the Texas Revolution. Originally it was part of Mexico and served as an important town during the revolution. However, the thick walls of the homes were originally designed to fend off frequent attacks from the Comanche.

Drive to the end of Grant Avenue until it dead-ends at the Rio Grande, park, and then walk to the gate to the right. There is usually a friendly member of the Border Patrol stationed by the river if you need directions. The San Ygnacio Bird Sanctuary isn't grand by any means, but it does offer a birding platform, blind, drip, and a few shaded benches where you can sit and watch the ribbon of green along the river light up with color during the migrations. This is also where White-collared Seedeaters and Varied Buntings occasionally hop across the Rio Grande and send birders all aflutter.

From March to May watch for Altamira, Audubon's, Bullock's, Hooded, and Orchard Orioles, while Verdins, Yellow-breasted Chats, and Green Jays are all common sightings from April to June. The river is a good place to listen and look for Belted, Ringed, and Green Kingfishers fishing alongside the Anhingas and Ospreys. The river also serves as a superhighway for gulls, terns, and shorebirds as they move north and south on migration routes that are as old as the river itself. The small platform is a good place to search the skies for Cooper's, Gray, Harris's, Red-shouldered, and Swainson's Hawks during the spring and fall migrations. The volunteers maintain a few drips and feeding stations that bring in Black-crested Titmice, Morelet's Seedeaters, and a passel of doves.

When you do visit, make sure to pack a lunch and water if you plan on visiting for a few hours, as the town is light on services. Even though it can feel like you are a million miles from somewhere, there is often other birders and volunteers milling about. This sanctuary is a great example of a handful of concerned citizens getting together to set aside a few acres of conservation lands where people can observe and enjoy the birds. The sanctuary is north of Falcon Lake State Park and is part of the Zapata Loop on the Texas Parks and Wildlife Great Texas Coastal Birding Trail.

⫸ Feather Fact ⫷

Long-billed Thrasher: If I were to name this thrasher, I would call it the Long-songed Thrasher; the complex song of the males seems to be much longer than their curved bill. During the spring look to the tops of trees for the males as they serenade the females. They are a resident of the brush country of South Texas and Mexico, where they can be found foraging on the ground for insects, spiders, snails, and berries.

FIGURE 8.19. Long-billed Thrasher (photo by Jennifer L. Bristol).

9 • Trans-Pecos

NEW MEXICO

Odessa

Monahans

Pecos

Pecos R.

Fort Stockton

Rio Grande

⑤

④

Fort Davis

③

Alpine

①

MEXICO

②

Terlingua

0   20 miles

TRANS-PECOS REGION
KEY:
1   Gage Hotel and Gardens
2   Big Bend National Park
3   Chihuahuan Desert Research Institute
4   Lawrence E. Wood/Madera Canyon Roadside Park
5   Balmorhea State Park
6   Guadalupe Mountains National Park: Frijole Ranch

FIGURE 9.1. Curve-billed Thrasher (photo by Jennifer L. Bristol).

FIGURE 9.2. Male Scott's Oriole (photo by Jennifer L. Bristol).

FIGURE 9.3. Wilson's Snipe (photo by Jennifer L. Bristol).

FIGURE 9.4. Male Bullock's Oriole (photo by Jennifer L. Bristol).

Texas Parks and Wildlife Department defines West Texas as the Trans-Pecos region. For most people, West Texas is a place where it's hard to pull fact from fiction and tall tales can easily be as true as the sunset. Ecologically speaking, the area is defined by the only place in Texas where there are both desert and mountains. The limited rainfall, less than twelve inches a year, gives rise to hardy plants that can survive with little water and tolerate the extreme heat and cold temperatures. According to Texas Parks and Wildlife, the Trans-Pecos area is around twenty-four million acres with more than 268 species of native grasses and 447 species of woody plants.

Ecosystems can change rapidly when elevation and water enter the mix. The birds of the region are also different from those in other parts of the state. Even though West Texas is still considered to be squarely in the Central Flyway, it attracts birds that are better suited to living in the arid mountains, deserts, or high plains. There are also frequent visitors from the Pacific Flyway that cross over state lines and give Texas birders fits of excitement. Several species of birds are considered West Texas specialties and can be found only along the Rio Grande wetlands, in the foothills of the mountains, or in the desert meadows.

The people here are as sparse as the rain. Water is hard to come by to sustain large populations, which is part of the allure. When traveling in the area, it is best to be self-sufficient. Don't let your car get close to empty in those vast empty spaces, and pack extra water even for short day trips.

Gage Hotel and Gardens (192 species)
106 First Street, Marathon, TX 79842
http://gagehotel.com
Parking Lot, Short Trail

If you are staying at the Gage Hotel in Marathon, it is worth the time to walk across the railroad tracks to the romantic garden. The small oasis has been completely contrived but is splendid nonetheless. The mile-long walking trail meanders through grassy lawns, rose beds, native plants, a small pond, and even a putting green, all under the canopy of several majestic cottonwoods. As you pass through the garden in the spring look for Black-chinned Hummingbirds, Bell's Vireos, House Finchs, Verminllion Flycatchers, and Golden-fronted Woodpeckers. If the gates are closed to the gardens, the birding from the parking lot is still pretty decent.

The space is peaceful and relaxing even on a hot, dry spring day. When I visited in April, I was treated to the lovely, melodic song of the White-crowned Sparrow, which mixed in harmony with the wind whispering through the cottonwoods. I drank in the moment before regrouping with my birding team to press on to find more species. One of the most memorable birds that went soaring overhead was the Zone-tailed Hawk. Its flight was silent as it passed not too far from the ground, flashing its distinctive fanned tail; then it twisted on the wind for a moment and perched on top of the old windmill.

I find the town of Marathon fascinating. As I strolled the empty streets to bird, I also did some self-reflection and concluded I am a lucky lady indeed. I am grateful for not being an early settler trying to eke out a living from the rocky, thorny, dry land of the region. Instead, I indulged in a wonderful meal at the Gage Hotel with my family and slept comfortably in a temperature-controlled room.

FIGURE 9.5. Male and female House Finches (photo by Jennifer L. Bristol).

Big Bend National Park (450 species)
310 Alsate Road, Big Bend National Park, TX 79834
https://www.nps.gov/bibe/index.htm
Parking Lots, Campgrounds, Short Trails

Big Bend is one of my favorite places in Texas but difficult to get to. No matter how you slice it, the park is a long way from anywhere. However, its remote location is what makes it a special place to visit. The diversity of habitat attracts a wide range of birds and wildlife that inhabit the park and adjacent Big Bend Ranch State Park. From the canyons and wetlands surrounding the mighty Rio Grande to the lofty heights of the Chisos Mountains, the landscape is simultaneously breathtaking and intimidating.

When we were dating, my husband and I took our first long trip together to Big Bend. I knew he was a keeper when his idea of a romantic getaway was to backpack and camp the South Rim. We laughed our faces off, and I'm pretty sure I decided I wanted to hitch my wagon to his team for the long haul on that trip.

What I also discovered on that trip was that the parking lots at the Chisos Basin Visitor Center, Window View Trail, and Chisos Basin Campground offer some amazing birding. Western birds such as the Chihuahuan Raven, Mexican Jay, Cactus Wren, and Curve-billed and Crissal Thrasher all arrive in the area. I never get tired of hearing the lonely song of the Cactus Wren; it sounds like pure Texas to me.

The trees in the Basin offer good habitat for Acorn and Ladder-backed Woodpeckers and the lovely Northern Flickers. The pinyon-juniper-oak woodlands also draw in the Elf, Great Horned, and Western Screech-Owls, and the Mexican Whip-poor-will can be heard in the evening during the summer months after the sun goes down. Keep your eyes to the skies around Casa Grande Peak for a pair of Golden Eagles that occasionally visit the park.

The tiniest birds are the true stars of the show in this vast landscape. The Black-chinned, Broad-tailed, Lucifer, and Blue-throated Hummingbirds all swarm around the Basin, feeding from a number of flowering plants and cacti. The tiny birds flash their bold colors as they engage in air battles over nectar-giving plants or in courtship of the females. The greatest concentrations of hummers occur in late summer and early fall during their fall migration.

Drive down to the Rio Grande and stop at the Rio Grande Village Campground for a completely different birding experience. There is a wetland that brings in a surprising number of waterfowl and shorebirds, including Mexican Ducks, Soras, Wilson's Snipe, and Spotted Sandpipers. The temperature can change dramatically as you descend from the mountains to the valley floor, so make sure you take plenty of water and know your limits. The vegetation and habitat change dramatically as well, and with the change comes a transformation in the avian life. Birds like Cordilleran and

Vermilion Flycatchers, Black and Say's Phoebes, Pyrrhuloxias, and Plumbeous Vireos are all present even in the heat of the summer. The tiny Black-tailed Gnatcatcher can be found flashing about after aphids year-round along the Rio Grande. I do not recommend visiting the valleys of Big Bend in the summer unless you enjoy face-searing heat. Spring is easier on the face and can bring Lark and Lazuli Buntings, Gray and Blue-headed Vireos, Canyon and Spotted Towhees, and Scaled Quail.

Throughout the park you will find a stunning array of raptors. Rio Grande Village has a nesting area for the Common Black Hawk, whose preferred habitat is mature cottonwood trees near water. The best time to see the Common Black Hawk and other raptors such as the Gray, Swainson's, and Zone-tailed Hawks is between March and September.

Visiting Big Bend takes some effort, but it is worth it. If you want to stay at the lodge, plan your dates early and stick to them because reservations are difficult to obtain. Alternatively, you can bring your RV or pitch a tent in the campgrounds, but those reservations also book quickly. Sitting under the blanket of stars in the remote Chisos Basin is the perfect place to unplug and reset your mind after a full day of birding and exploring.

⟫ Feather Fact ⟪

Cactus Wren: Here's how you can find a Cactus Wren: visit the Southwest, look for a cactus, and find the wren. The song of this wren is often used in movies to indicate that the scene is set in the Southwest. When these busy little birds aren't singing, they are constructing their own nests, destroying another bird's nests, or hopping along the ground after a bug. Like several other desert birds they can acquire all the water they need from the insects and berries they consume. It's always fun to see them take a dust bath in the evening, another behavior they have adopted due to the scarcity of water in their range. These birds are in sharp decline due to habitat loss and removal of cacti.

FIGURE 9.6. Cactus Wren at Big Bend National Park (photo by Jennifer L. Bristol).

Chihuahuan Desert Research Institute (147 species)
43869 TX 118, Fort Davis, TX 79734
http://www.cdri.org
Parking Lot, Nature Center Campus, Short Trail

This small but important nature center is located just south of Fort Davis and offers a window into the avian world that lives in the vastness of the region. The trails are pretty rugged and might be considered strenuous by most folk's standards. However, the Hummingbird Trail that loops around the Botanical Gardens is worth a visit during the spring or summer. Rufous and Broad-tailed Hummingbirds frequent the gardens from July to October, and Calliope, Anna's, and Lucifer Hummingbirds pass through on occasion.

The grounds of the nature center have plenty of birds to observe almost year-round. From May to October it is common to find Cassin's Kingbirds, Cassin's Finches, and Cassin's Sparrows as well as Brewer's Sparrows and Phainopeplas. During the winter, flocks of Dark-eyed Juncos and Pyrrhuloxias can be seen feeding on the ground or sitting in the low shrubs.

The center provides valuable research about the plants, wildlife, and habitat of the Chihuahuan Desert and Trans-Pecos region. It offers guided nature walks and recently opened a new birding blind. Check the website for hours of operation and entrance fees.

≫ **Feather Fact** ≪

Summer Tanager: Male Summer Tanagers are the only all-red birds in North America, and the females are a more subdued yellow. Both are pretty to look at and have an equally lovely song that can be heard in open woodlands, where they prefer to nest. They feed on insects and fruit, with a special affinity for bees and wasps. Once they capture an insect, they thrash it against a branch to get rid of the stinger before consuming it. When mulberries or blackberries are ripe, it is common to find these birds feasting on the fruits. They breed in much of Texas where pine or oak forests exist.

FIGURE 9.7. Male Summer Tanager (photo by Jennifer L. Bristol).

Lawrence E. Wood/Madera Canyon Roadside Park (203 species)

Madera Canyon Roadside Park, Fort Davis, TX 79734
www.treksw.com/madera-canyon-trail-davis-mountains/
Parking Lot, Short Trail

At Kent, take Highway 118 south from I-10 to Fort Davis. As the road winds its way up the foothills into the Davis Mountains, you will come across a roadside park and picnic area where it is worthwhile to stop. The park is near the Nature Conservancy's thirty-three thousand–acre Davis Mountain Preserve, but most important, it is high in elevation and provides access to birds you might not otherwise see. It is also the parking area for the Madera Canyon Trail, which is absolutely stunning in the spring and early summer when the flowers are blooming.

This is a good place to see Scaled and Montezuma Quail or Wild Turkeys strolling along with their families. From April to September Anna's, Black-chinned, Broad-tailed, and Rufous Hummingbirds flash past as they move from flower to perch. During the same time check the skies for Common and Lesser Nighthawks, Common Poorwills, Mexican Whip-poor-wills, and White-throated Swifts. Summer also brings in Hepatic, Summer, and Western Tanagers, as well as Black-headed and Blue Grosbeaks. From October to March it is easy to find Williamson's and Red-naped Sapsuckers, Brewer's Sparrows, and Loggerheaded Shrikes mixing it up with resident birds such as Acorn Woodpeckers, Common Ravens, and White-breasted Nuthatches.

Birding in the Davis Mountains is exciting, as it yields such a variety of birds that exist only in this part of the state. If you do plan to venture out on the Madera Canyon Trail, make sure you have plenty of water and know your limits. The trail can be rugged but is worth the effort.

⋙ Feather Fact ⋘

Wild Turkey: This large game bird was one of the many gifts the New World yielded to the first wave of Europeans. The bird has been a popular dinner item since the 1500s and saw a serious decline in population in the early 1900s as the human populations increased across the United States. Conservation efforts helped stabilize the population. Females raise and care for the chicks and often band together with other broods to form large flocks during the winter. Even though they are not great flyers, they will hop up into trees to roost and are fairly efficient swimmers.

FIGURE 9.8. Male Wild Turkey (photo by Jennifer L. Bristol).

Balmorhea State Park (239 species)
9207 TX 17, Toyahvale, TX 79786
https://tpwd.texas.gov/state-parks/balmorhea
Parking Lot, Campground, Short Trail

There are oases in the world, and then there is Balmorhea State Park and San Solomon Springs. Surrounded by the mighty Chihuahuan Desert, the springs are a welcome sight on any day. The park is only forty-five acres with the main feature being the spring-fed pool, which is roughly 1.4 acres and holds 3.5 million gallons of clear, refreshing water. Built between 1936 and 1941 by the Civilian Conservation Corps, the pool and park have served as a welcome resting stop for travelers for more than seventy years.

There is a restored wetland that has a nice pavilion near the wetlands where you can watch the birds. The wetlands, tall trees along the springs, and scrub grasslands are where most of the action takes place in the park. The birding is surprisingly good here year-round because of the abundance of water.

This is a good spot to find Prairie Falcons, Northern Harriers, and Cooper's Hawks working the fields for sparrows, mice, lizards, and snakes. Brewer's, Black-throated, Black-chinned, Rufous-crowned, and Savannah Sparrows are all frequent flyers to the area. Because of the wetlands, you will also find Least, Spotted, and Solitary Sandpipers; Black-crowned and Yellow-crowned Night-Herons; and the ever-present American Coot.

I've seen the Phainopepla only a few times, and this is one of the places to find this unusual bird. It looks like a black Northern Cardinal with striking red eyes. Speaking of things that look like Cardinals, this is also a good location to see the Pyrrhuloxia.

Just north of the state park is Balmorhea Lake, which is frequented by a number of ducks and geese during the winter months.

⋙ Feather Fact ⋘

Northern Harrier: Like most raptors the female is larger than the male, but both have the distinctive white rump. It's not hard to identify this medium-sized hawk, as it can be found effortlessly soaring low over fields and marshes as it looks for rodents and other birds. Unlike most hawks Northern Harriers use sound and sight to locate prey and are constantly listening for movement in the reeds and grasses as they silently pass overhead. They can be found across Texas during the fall and winter before heading to the upper Midwest and Canada for the spring and summer breeding season.

FIGURE 9.9. Northern Harrier (photo by Jennifer L. Bristol).

Guadalupe Mountains National Park:
Frijole Ranch (183 species)
400 Pine Canyon, Salt Flat, TX 79847
https://www.nps.gov/gumo/planyourvisit/frijole.htm
Parking Lot, Short Trail

One of the things I like the most about this place is the silence. The remote old ranch sits at the base of the Guadalupe Mountains along a natural spring. The wind coming down the hillside, brushing lightly through the sparse trees around the ranch house, and the quick flitter of birds are about the only sounds you will hear if you sit quietly and listen to the conversations of nature.

Frijole Ranch is not a birding buffet like some other stops, but it offers some rather unique Trans-Pecos birds. I recommend strolling along the path that leads from the parking lot to the ranch house and cultural center. You will find most of the birds in the trees and scrub brush surrounding the springs. For more viewing, you can press on farther down the quarter-mile ADA-accessible path to Manzanita Spring and oasis.

This is one of the few locations where you can find Hepatic, Summer, and Western Tanagers and Varied and Painted Buntings during the summer months. Summer is a good time to visit Guadalupe Mountains National Park, but fall and spring are best.

My husband and I took a road trip for our honeymoon that included a stop at Frijole Ranch. We hiked up the short 2.3-mile Smith Spring Loop Trail to the tiny oasis of twisting big-tooth maples and Texas madrones that encircle the spring. Nestled in the fairy-like grove are Green-tailed Towhees; Pyrrhuloxias; and Cordilleran, Olive-sided, and Hammond's Flycatchers. We had just missed the peak of the fall colors on that trip, but it is on our list to return one day to witness that natural wonder.

Pyrrhuloxia: This bird is closely related to the Northern Cardinal but is more gray than red and has a large yellow bill. Pyrrhuloxias' well-developed bill supports them in being an opportunistic omnivore well suited for the blistering heat of the Southwest and northern Mexico desert scrub country. They can obtain most of the fluids they require from eating insects and drinking plant nectar when water is scarce. During the winter, when hawks return to the area, Pyrrhuloxias form into large social flocks of up to one thousand birds for safety.

FIGURE 9.10. Male Pyrrhuloxia (photo by Jennifer L. Bristol).

10 • Lubbock and
the Panhandle

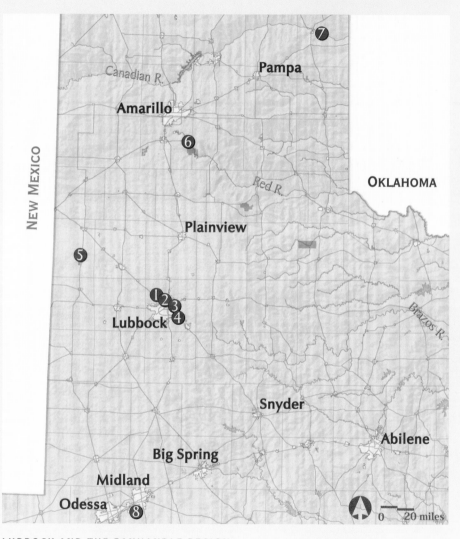

LUBBOCK AND THE PANHANDLE REGION
KEY:
1   Lubbock Lake National Historic Landmark
2   Buddy Holly Recreation Area
3   Mackenzie Park and Simmons Park
4   Buffalo Springs Lake and Lake Ransom Canyon
5   Muleshoe National Wildlife Refuge
6   Palo Duro Canyon State Park
7   Lake Marvin and Gene Howe Wildlife Management Area
8   I-20 Wildlife Preserve and Jenna Welch Nature Study Center

FIGURE 10.1. Canada Geese on frozen lake in Lubbock (photo by Jennifer L. Bristol).

FIGURE 10.2. Sandhill Cranes on the wing (photo by Jennifer L. Bristol).

The Texas Panhandle comprises two ecoregions: the High Plains and the Rolling Plains. For the most part, the birding locations mentioned here are in the High Plains where large flocks of wintering waterfowl still gather in the playa lakes from November to March. The area was once dominated by shortgrass prairies, but after water was discovered under the Caprock in the Ogallala Aquifer, the region became dominated by agricultural lands.

Another liquid commodity lurks beneath the thin soil: oil. The region struck it rich with oil in the 1920s and has continued to be one of the most productive oil fields in the world. When visiting the area, make sure you scan the pumpjacks for hawks and vultures. If the jacks aren't pumping, the hawks will often perch on them to scan for a tasty meal of prairie dog, jackrabbit, or lizard.

The Panhandle can have extreme weather from cold, windy winters to hot, windy summers. The one thing that is consistent all year round is the wind. However, if you like wide-open spaces with skies filled with flocks of geese and Sandhill Cranes, there is no better place than the High Plains on a cool day in December.

FIGURE 10.3. American Coot (photo by Jennifer L. Bristol).

Lubbock City Parks (Multiple Stops)

Did you know that Lubbock has more than seventy-five parks, and the birding in the area is really good from fall to spring? On the arid Caprock area, water is like gold. There is one watershed worth exploring in detail: Yellow House Draw, which flows into the North Fork of the Double Mountain Fork of the Brazos River. The Brazos River? It's true; the headwaters of the mighty Brazos River flow out of the Caprock all the way to College Station to an area just west of Houston and into the Gulf of Mexico. How cool would it be to bird the entire watershed of the mighty river?

Lubbock Lake National Historic Landmark (165 species)

2401 Landmark Drive, Lubbock, TX 79415
www.depts.ttu.edu/museumttu/lll/
Parking Lot, Nature Center Campus, Short Trail

Our journey along the watershed starts at a place that was the end for many pre-historic animals and birds: the Lubbock Lake National Historic Landmark. Yellow House Draw began in this area around twenty thousand years ago and has been transforming the region ever since. This location is a nature center, museum, research lab, and park that is part of Texas Tech University.

Leading away from the parking lot is a nice ADA interpretive trail that winds through the restored prairie area. Best in late fall to late spring, this area is home to Burrowing Owls, too many sparrows to list, American Goldfinches, Cooper's Hawks, American Kestrels, and Northern Bobwhites. If you don't have time to make a lap around the one-mile archeology trail, you can bird from the parking lot and have pretty good luck spotting several species, especially the large flocks of passing geese and Sandhill Cranes.

⧉ Feather Fact ⧉

Western Meadowlark: This festive yellow, black, and tan bird is a year-round resident of the Texas Panhandle. Look for Western Meadowlarks in fields and grasslands across the western part of the United States or for males singing joyfully atop a bush or fence post. Their melodic song is like a tonic that can simply dissolve away a bad day. The Eastern Meadowlark is a little bit flashier, but the Western can boast being the state bird of six states.

FIGURE 10.4. Western Meadowlark (photo by Jennifer L. Bristol).

Buddy Holly Recreation Area (116 species)
Canyon Lake Drive, Lubbock, TX 79415
https://ci.lubbock.tx.us/departments/parks-recreation/parks/lubbock-parks
Parking Lots, Short Trails

Across Highway 289 from the Lubbock Lake National Historic Landmark along Canyon Drive is the Buddy Holly Recreation Area. When the ducks and geese are wintering in the area, the place is noisy with birds. On one winter birding expedition to this location, I watched a giant Ferruginous Hawk swoop down over a gaggle of Canada and Cackling Geese, using them as cover, so he could snatch a prairie dog for a meal from the banks on the other side of the small lake. As he soared in on his raid, the geese dove for cover underwater (which I had never seen them do before) and flew in every possible direction, squawking all the while.

The small park has a pavilion next to the parking lot, which is a pleasant place to relax and enjoy the birds. The ADA-accessible trails create short loops around the lake and offer good vantage points for viewing waterfowl or White-breasted Nuthatches, Northern Flickers, and Ladder-backed Woodpeckers in the sparse trees.

>>> **Feather Fact** <<<

Canada Goose: Flocks of these large geese love to travel in a V formation both in flight and on the water. There are eleven subspecies of this common goose, which include the smaller Cackling Goose. All subspecies share the distinctive black head and neck and white chinstrap. Because of changes in climate and agricultural practices, many Canada Geese choose not to migrate for breeding. Migrants winter in the southern parts of the United States and travel north to Canada and the Arctic Circle to breed. Young geese stay with their parents for a full year and wait until they are around four years old to breed. The oldest documented Canada Goose was thirty-three years old.

FIGURE 10.5.
Canada Geese at the Buddy Holly Recreation Area (photo by Jennifer L. Bristol).

Mackenzie Park (210 species) and
Mae Simmons Park (180 species),
600 Cesar East Chavez Drive, Lubbock, TX 7940
https://ci.lubbock.tx.us/departments/parks-recreation/parks/lubbock-parks
Parking Lots, Short Trails

These parks flow together as they follow Yellow House Draw. Mackenzie and Simmons Parks offer some of the easiest parking lot birding in the state. Just drive up, angle your car so you can see the lake, and pull out your optics.

Yellow House Draw and Dunbar Historical Lake attract ducks in the fall and winter months, such as Buffleheads, Common Goldeneyes, Northern Shovelers, and Blue- and Green-winged Teals. I've spotted Hooded, Common, and Red-breasted Mergansers, as well as Horned, Eared, and Pied-billed Grebes along the calm waters of Dunbar Lake. From October to March it is common to see Song Sparrows, Dark-eyed Juncos, Western Meadowlarks, Eastern Bluebirds, American Goldfinches, and Marsh Wrens dancing through the prairie grasses and reeds near the lake. As spring arrives, so do Western Kingbirds, Barn Swallows, Mississippi Kites, and Spotted Sandpipers. Some of the year-round residents include Belted Kingfishers, Blue Jays, American Robins, and Red-Winged Blackbirds.

All of these stops are city parks and well maintained. However, they can get hot, as they have little to no shade, so be sure to pack water if you plan to explore the trails during warm weather.

Ruddy Duck: When I look at Ruddy Ducks, I think of one word: *bold.* The males swim around with their tail up and their deep chestnut-brown chest out. The male's bill turns a brilliant blue during breeding season. Unlike most ducks, they wait to pair up until they reach their breeding grounds in the Rio Grande Valley, playa lakes in Texas, or the Great Plains. Females lay large eggs, which results in a more developed duckling when it hatches. Each egg takes a lot of energy to produce and can be almost 12 percent of a female's body weight. Adults and ducklings are shallow divers that will eat just about any crustacean or insect the marsh has to offer.

FIGURE 10.6. Male Ruddy Duck (photo by Jennifer L. Bristol).

Buffalo Springs Lake and Lake Ransom Canyon (246 species)
9999 High Meadow Road, Buffalo Springs, TX 79404
https://buffalospringslake.net
Parking Lots, Campground

Follow the same watershed to Buffalo Springs Lake and Lake Ransom Canyon. Trust me, you won't be sorry you made the journey. I was completely surprised when I discovered this oasis on the edge of the Caprock. The combination of water and canyons, with fields above, makes a perfect haven for wintering waterfowl as well as spring and fall migrants. The expansive parking lot at the marina offers a large area of paved square footage to bird. Both lakes are filled with ducks, geese, mergansers, and shorebirds of all varieties.

The canyon surrounding the campground is worth taking the time to look for warblers and woodpeckers during the day or listening for the Great Horned Owl in the evening. Just east of the dam is a parking lot that juts out into the lake and offers a good spot to see Ospreys, Franklin's Gulls, Forster's Terns, and Belted Kingfishers.

⚛ Feather Fact ⚛

Great Horned Owl: This large raptor can take down much larger prey, such as Ospreys, but feeds mostly on rodents, frogs, and even bats. Other birds such as crows and mockingbirds will mob these owls for hours and with good reason; the owls are a common predator. Their strong talons are used to sever the spine of their prey as they silently swoop in to snatch it up. They have soft, lightweight feathers that add to their stealth and allow them to be adaptive to cold climates. Like most owls, they can turn their head 180 degrees to see in all directions.

FIGURE 10.7.
Great Horned Owl
(photo by Jennifer
L. Bristol).

Muleshoe National Wildlife Refuge (237 species)

1531 County Road 1248, Muleshoe, TX 79347
https://www.fws.gov/refuge/muleshoe/
Parking Lot, Short Trail, Bird Blind, Scenic Overlook

This place is cool for many reasons. I was introduced to the refuge in the early 1990s while visiting a boyfriend's family. The relationship didn't last, and I must confess, I had a harder time breaking up with his parents than with him. The refuge, however, left a lifelong impression.

This place is remote and peaceful in a way that few places are. The sound of the wind blowing through the shortgrass prairie can make you feel lonesome and be comforting at the same time. This was the first national wildlife refuge set aside in Texas in 1935, and the prairies in the park have never been plowed or cultivated. If you look on the Google Maps satellite image, you will understand why that is significant. The refuge is best known for hosting the largest concentration of wintering Sandhill Cranes in the United States. From December to February the refuge can host as many as 250,000 Sandhills.

It is a treat to watch the giant, graceful birds return from feeding in the fields to the safety of the playa lakes at sunset. They slowly soar above the playa and make a circular safety check before landing and greeting the other gathering families. In that moment, and if no one else is there, the only sounds you will hear are the wind, the birds, and yourself. On a peaceful day in December my husband and I visited Goose Lake to watch thousands of Sandhills gather. On other trips I've had great luck watching the birds at Paul's Lake, where the viewing area consists of only a parking lot, pit toilet, and birding platform. This location is also home to shorebirds, ducks, geese, and too many sparrows to list. Meadowlarks, Curve-billed Thrashers, Scaled Quail, Northern Bobwhites, and Dark-eyed Juncos are also common here.

If you like raptors, this will be a birding bonanza for you. Rough-legged, Ferruginous, and Swainson's Hawks mix with the Peregrine and Prairie Falcons, Common Nighthawks, and an occasional Golden Eagle, which all feed on the snakes, lizards, small mammals, moths, and even the other small birds of the High Plains. The area surrounding the refuge headquarters is best for spotting a resident Great Horned Owl.

Even though I love visiting in the winter, May can also be a prime time for bird viewing in this region. The trees near the headquarters and parking area are a great place to see migrating Yellow, Wilson's, and Yellow-rumped Warblers; Blue Grosbeaks; and Bullock's Orioles. Between March and September and if there is water in the playas, look for Snowy Plovers, American Avocets, Wilson's Phalaropes, and Great Blue Herons.

Morning and evening, when the lighting is subtle, are also the best times to take photos. The wide-open plains of the Caprock can get bright in the afternoon sun, which makes it harder to take good wildlife photos.

⋙ **Feather Fact** ⋘

Sandhill Crane: Fossil records date this bird back about 2.5 million years. When you see these large wading birds, it's hard not to think of dinosaurs or something ancient. They are known for their elaborate and even romantic courtship displays used to find and maintain a mate. They mate for life after reaching breeding age at around seven years old. They can live up to thirty years and will travel more than one hundred thousand miles in their lifetime. These large birds winter in Texas but migrate to northern Canada and the Arctic Circle during the breeding season. They are considered a game bird and are hunted during certain seasons. A group is called a construction, dance, or sedge.

FIGURE 10.8. Sandhill Cranes (photo by Jennifer L. Bristol).

Palo Duro Canyon State Park (246 species)

11450 State Highway Park Road 5, Canyon, TX 79015
https://tpwd.texas.gov/state-parks/palo-duro-canyon
Parking Lots, Campgrounds, Short Trails

If you drive from Austin, it seems to take forever to get to Palo Duro Canyon State Park. However, the reward is worth the effort. The dramatic cliffs along the canyon, the oasis along the creek, and the variety of birds are all part of the pageantry of this special place. Humans have inhabited the canyon for about twelve thousand years. The earliest people, the Clovis and Folsom, hunted mammoth and giant bison in the canyon. The early Spanish explorers gave it the name Palo Duro for the hard wood they found there.

However, the Comanche who lived in the canyon part of the year interest me the most. They were masterful equestrians and could ride like the wind across Texas on their sturdy mustangs. They often evaded the US Army and Texas Rangers by slipping into the vastness of the second-largest canyon system in the United States and disappearing from sight. If you are going to visit the area, check out *Empire of the Summer Moon* by S. C. Gwynne to learn more about the history of the most powerful tribe that once called Texas home.

Because the canyon is carved out of the vast plains of the Caprock, it offers birds a protected area from the ever-present winds and provides water opportunities. It is a good place to look for Chipping, Field, Fox, Lincoln's, Savannah, Vesper, White-crowned, and White-throated Sparrows, which are all common from fall to early spring. The brush thickets are alive with ground birds such as Wild Turkeys, Curve-billed and Brown Thrashers, Eastern Meadowlarks, and Gambel's Quail. American Robins spend time in here too but are often mistaken for their close relative, the towhees. Green-tailed, Spotted, and Canyon Towhees all like to scratch along the ground near the brush thickets.

I've had the best luck with spotting a great variety of birds from the Hackberry Campground loop. However, you will find a nice variety of birds year-round anywhere along the creek or near the big trees. If you plan on camping in the park, I recommend making your reservations at least thirty days in advance. Even in July we had a hard time getting an RV campsite at this popular state park.

Northern Bobwhite: This dapper little quail lives in social groups known as coveys. At night Northern Bobwhites roost by circling up with their tails facing the center of the circle and their keen dark eyes facing outward to keep watch. They make a tasty treat for just about any grassland predator, from owls to snakes to feral cats to humans, which makes them ever vigilant. They have long been an economic engine of the game-bird hunting industry, and their sharp population decline in recent decades has had an impact on that sport. The reasons for their decline are not fully understood, but the National Bobwhite Conservation Initiative is working hard to understand the factors to get conservation plans in place.

FIGURE 10.9 Northern Bobwhite (photo by Jennifer L. Bristol).

Lake Marvin (205 species) and Gene Howe
Wildlife Management Area (164)
FM 2266, Canadian, TX 79014
http://canadiantx.org/index.php/resources/area-attractions/black-kettle-na-tional-grasslands-lake-marvin
Parking Lot, Short Trail

Up in the High Plains region along the Canadian River, just down the road from the interesting little town of Canadian, are Lake Marvin and the Gene Howe Wildlife Management Area. Both are a mix of sand sage and shortgrass rangeland with taller grasses and cottonwoods along the bottomlands.

The wildlife management area is an interesting place to wander around, but I find Lake Marvin a little easier to bird. The Old Military Road Campground and parking lot has picnic tables where you can hang out, and there is a short trail and boardwalk that lead down to the lake. Both areas are good spots to find Lark, Indigo, and Painted Buntings in late May. During April it is common to see Harris's, Lincoln's, Song, White-crowned, and Vesper Sparrows along with Spotted and Eastern Towhees. Snow and Canada Geese, Canvasbacks, Northern Pintails, and Sandhill Cranes show up in droves from November to March, while Red-headed, Red-bellied, Hairy, and Downy Woodpeckers pound away during the summer months.

Both places are remote but easy to access from the little town of Canadian, which is about two hours from Amarillo. The habitat does support the endangered Lesser Prairie-Chicken, but this bird is very elusive and more often sighted on private lands.

White-crowned Sparrow: This otherwise brown-and-buff sparrow wears a jaunty black-and-white crown. These sparrows winter across most of the central and southern parts of the United States and into Mexico, and they migrate to northern Canada and Alaska to breed during the summer. According to the Cornell Lab of Ornithology, these long-distance migrators can travel up to three hundred miles in one night. Wherever they go, they take along their lovely, distinctive song, which they learn from their flock rather than their parents.

FIGURE 10.10. White-crowned Sparrow (photo by Jennifer L. Bristol).

I-20 Wildlife Preserve and Jenna Welch Nature Study Center (233 species)
2201 South Midland Drive, Midland, TX 79703
https://www.i20wp.org
Parking Lot, Short Trail, Bird Blind, Boardwalk, Observation Platform

When you think about all the places to bird, Midland might not cross your mind. However, the concerned citizens who help conserve and develop the eighty-seven acres of the I-20 Wildlife Preserve and Jenna Welch Nature Study Center sure have. You might recognize the name, Jenna Welch, as she is the mother of former First Lady Laura Bush. She was a birding enthusiast and believer in the transformative power nature holds in the education of children.

Just past the oil pumpjack, the preserve parking lot looks north toward a grove of large trees and the playa, which are usually filled with migrants. If the gates are closed, the birding is still pretty good in the fields and habitat that surround the parking area. The short trail and boardwalk lead to several nice bird blinds that look out over the playa lake. Ducks are the stars of the show at this location. From December to May look for Wood Ducks, Cinnamon Teals, Gadwalls, American Wigeons, and Canvasbacks. Some waterfowl stay year-round, such as Ruddy Ducks and Mallards, American Coots, and Pied-billed Grebes. The playa also produces a fair amount of bugs, which the flycatchers and warblers enjoy during the spring and fall migrations.

Not far from the preserve a Snowy Owl was sighted during the winter of 2018. I searched in vain to find it. I'm still not sure what the young female owl was thinking when she took up residence along the busy highway between Midland and Odessa at the discount auto parts center. The land around the area is pretty devoid of tall trees or the normal habitat that the owls prefer. A local birder told me that this was not the first time a Snowy Owl has drifted so far south. The birder also speculated that the intense fires that had plagued the western states and Canada that year might have sent a variety of birds in search of habitat that was not burned to a crisp. I can't confirm that information is true, but it sounds reasonable.

Gadwall: At first this medium-sized down duck might seem a little dull compared to the more flamboyant Mallard or American Wigeon. The Gadwall is a study in the fine details of black and brown tones with a single white patch on the male's wing. Gadwalls winter across Texas and most of the southern states and into Mexico and migrate north into the Great Plains and Canada to nest and breed. Populations were once quite low, but they have made a strong comeback thanks to conservation efforts to protect and restore wetlands, especially in the Great Plains. They can live up to nineteen years in the wild; however, they are the third most-hunted duck after Mallards and Green-winged Teals.

FIGURE 10.11. Gadwalls (photo by Thomas Nilles).

Bibliography

Publications

Carson, Rachel. Silent Spring. Boston: Houghton Mifflin, 1962.

Clark, Gary. Book of Texas Birds. College Station: Texas A&M University Press, 2016.

Haenn, William F. Fort Clark and Brackettville. Mount Pleasant, SC: Arcadia Publishing, 2002.

Johnson, William P., and Mark W. Lockwood. Texas Waterfowl. College Station: Texas A&M University Press, 2013.

Kyle, Paul, and Georgean Kyle. Chimney Swifts: American's Mysterious Birds above the Fireplace. College Station: Texas A&M University Press, 2005.

Lockwood, Mark W. Basic Texas Birds: A Field Guide. Austin: University of Texas Press, 2007.

Louv, Richard. Last Child in the Woods. Chapel Hill, NC: Algonquin Books of Chapel Hill, 2005.

Parker, Mary O. Explore Texas: A Nature Travel Guide. College Station: Texas A&M University Press, 2017.

Rising, James D. A Guide to the Identification and Natural History of the Sparrows of the United States and Canada. Cambridge, MA: Academic Press, 1996.

Sibley, David Allen. The Sibley Field Guide to Birds of Western North America. New York: Alfred A. Knopf, 2003.

———. The Sibley Guide to Birds. 2nd ed. New York: Alfred A. Knopf, 2014.

Smith-Rogers, Sheryl. "First Lady of Texas Birders." Texas Parks and Wildlife, May 2014. https://tpwmagazine.com/archive/2014/may/LLL_hagar/.

Stephenson, Tom, and Scott Whittle. The Warbler Guide. Princeton, NJ: Princeton University Press, 2015.

Todd, David, and Jonathan Ogren. The Texas Landscape Project: Nature and People. College Station: Texas A&M University Press, 2016.

Wernersbach, Julie, and Carolyn Tracy. The Swimming Holes of Texas. Austin: University of Texas Press, 2017.

Websites

"All about Birds." Cornell Lab of Ornithology, 2015. https://www.allaboutbirds.org.

"Anahuac National Wildlife Refuge." US Fish and Wildlife Service, last updated May 23, 2019. https://www.fws.gov/refuge/Anahuac.

"Attwater Prairie Chicken National Wildlife Refuge." US Fish and Wildlife Service, last updated March 20, 2019. https://www.fws.gov/refuge/attwater_prairie_chicken/.

Audubon Texas. January 2018. http://tx.audubon.org.

"Austin Parks and Recreation Department." City of Austin, April 2018. http://www.austintexas.gov/department/parks-and-recreation.

Balconies Canyon Conservation Plan. 2019. https://www.traviscountytx.gov/tnr/bccp.

"Berry Springs Park and Preserve." Williamson County, Texas, 2019. https://www.wilco.org/Departments/Parks-Recreation/County-Parks/Berry-Springs-Park.

"Birding Festivals and Events." Cornell Lab of Ornithology, May 1, 2019. https://www.allaboutbirds.org/birding-festivals/.

Buffalo Springs Lake. 2019. https://buffalospringslake.net.

Cibolo Nature Center and Farm. 2019. http://www.cibolo.org/about/.

Cook's Slough Sanctuary and Nature Park. 2017. https://www.visituvalde.com/uvalde_attrac-tions/cooks-slough-sanctuary-and-nature-park/.

"Corpus Christi Texas." HawkWatch International, 2014–18. https://hawkwatch.org/migration/item/82-corpus-christi-hawkwatch.

"Dancing Woodcock." YouTube, 2014. https://www.youtube.com/watch?v=jO27y_nOkWs&feature=youtu.be.

"Davis Mountains Preserve." The Nature Conservancy, 2019. https://www.nature.org/en-us/get-involved/how-to-help/places-we-protect/davis-mountains-preserve/.

eBird. June 2019. https://ebird.org/explore.

"Ellen Trout Zoo." City of Lufkin, December 2018. cityoflufkin.com/zoo/.

Fort Clark Springs. May 2019. https://www.fortclark.com.

Fort Worth Nature Center and Refuge. 2019. http://www.fwnaturecenter.org.

Friends of Copperfield Nature Trails. February 2019. https://www.copperfieldtrails.org.

Gage Hotel. 2018. http://gagehotel.com.

"Gene Howe WMA: Wildlife Viewing." Texas Parks and Wildlife Department, 2018. https://tpwd.texas.gov/huntwild/hunt/wma/find_a_wma/list/?id=8&activity=wildlifeViewing.

Granger Lake. 2019. https://www.recreation.gov/camping/gateways/515.

Houston Wilderness. 2019. http://houstonwilderness.org/about-ecoregions.

I-20 Wildlife Preserve. January 2018. https://www.i20wp.org.

John Bunker Sands Wetland Center. 2019. http://www.wetlandcenter.com.

"Laguna Atascosa National Wildlife Refuge." US Fish and Wildlife Service, last updated April 9, 2019. https://www.fws.gov/refuge/laguna_atascosa/.

"Muleshoe National Wildlife Refuge." US Fish and Wildlife Service, last updated January 5, 2018. https://www.fws.gov/refuge/Muleshoe/wildlife_and_habitat/index.html.

"Oso Bay Wetlands Preserve and Learning Center." Corpus Christi Parks and Recreation, May 2019. https://www.cctexas.com/services/general-government/oso-bay-wetlands-preserve-learning-center.

"Parks and Recreation." City of Lubbock, December 2018. https://ci.lubbock.tx.us/departments/parks-recreation.

Phil Hardberger Park Conservancy. May 2019. https://www.philhardbergerpark.org.

"Rare Bird Alert." Travis Audubon, February 2018. https://travisaudubon.org/category/rare-bird-alert.

Ratcliff Lake Recreation Area. Recreation.gov, 2019. https://www.fs.usda.gov/recarea/texas/recarea/?recid=30224.

"Sanctuaries." Houston Audubon, 2019. https://houstonaudubon.org/sanctuaries/.

SFA Gardens. Stephen F. Austin State University, October 2018. http://sfagardens.sfasu.edu.

South Padre Island Birding, Nature Center and Alligator Sanctuary. June 2019. https://www.spibirding.com/your-visit.

"State of North American Birds 2016." NABCI, Cornell Lab, 2019. http://www.stateofthebirds.org/2016.

Texas Ornithological Society. May 2019. http://www.texasbirds.org.

Texas Parks and Wildlife Department. June 2019. https://tpwd.texas.gov/huntwild/wildlife/wildlife-trails/.

"Texas State Parks." Texas Parks and Wildlife Department, last updated May 2019. https://tpwd.texas.gov/state-parks.

"TPWD Wildlife Districts." Texas Parks and Wildlife Department, December 2018. https://tpwd.texas.gov/landwater/land/habitats.

Travis County Parks. March 2019. https://parks.traviscountytx.gov.

"Whooping Cranes." US Fish and Wildlife Service, Aransas National Wildlife Refuge, last updated February 20, 2013. https://www.fws.gov/refuge/Aransas/wildlife/whooping_cranes.html.

"Wildlife Habitat." US Fish and Wildlife Service, Santa Ana National Wildlife Refuge, last updated May 14, 2013. https://www.fws.gov/refuge/Santa_Ana/wildlife_and_habitat.html.

"Woody Woodpecker." Wikipedia, last updated May 19, 2019. https://en.wikipedia.org/wiki/Woody_Woodpecker.

World Birding Center. 2010. http://www.theworldbirdingcenter.com.

"Worldwide Birding and Nature Tours." Victor Emanuel Nature Tours, last updated February 2019. https://ventbird.com.

Index

Cook's Slough Sanctuary and Nature Park, 113, 129
Cooper's Hawk, 61, 67, 141, 170, 184, 197, 205
Copperfield Nature Trail, 79, 109
Cordilleran Flycatchers, 191, 199
Cornell Lab of Ornithology, 4, 5, 48, 93, 104, 169
Corpus Christi, Texas, 136, 138, 141, 143, 145
Couch, Ed, 175
Couch's Kingbirds, 129, 131, 151, **160**, 172
Crescent Bend Nature Park, 113, 116
Crested Caracaras, 85, 86, 147, 175; feather fact, **117**
Crissal Thrashers, 191
Curve-billed Thrashers, 122, 173, **187**, 191, 211, 213

Dallas, Texas, 56, 58, 63, 65, 67, 75
Dallas: Joppa Preserve/ Lemmon Lake, 56, 65
Dallas-Fort Worth (DFW) Metropolis, 58, 69
Dark-eyed Junco, 89, 118, 193, 208, 211
Davis, John, 3
DDT, 28, 87, 93, 128, 146
Delta Lake Park, 159, 173
Devine Lake Park, 79, 96–97
Dickcissels, 65, 69, 124, 147
Doe Skin Ranch, 98–99
Dogwood Canyon Audubon Center, 56, 75, 77
Double-crested Cormorants, 18, 82; feather fact, **128**
Downy Woodpeckers, 59, 67, 77, 215
Dunlins, 147

Eared Grebes, 92, 126, 131, 139, 165, 208
Eastern Bluebirds, 20, 37, 86, 89, 208; feather fact **49**
Eastern Kingbirds, 69
Eastern Meadow Larks, 39, 86, 206, 213
Eastern Phoebes, **57**, 99, 118, 151, 177
Eastern Screech Owls, **44**, 175, 179
Eastern Towhees, 67, 94, 215
Eastern Wood-Peewees, 94, **137**, 151
eBird, 5, 22, 28, 31, 105, 175
ecoregions: Coastal Bend, 136, 138; Edwards Plateau, 81, 94, 98, 106, 115, 122; Great Plains, 7, 30, 35, 62, 156, 218; Gulf Coast Prairies and Marshes, 7, 17, 138; High Plains, 203, 211, 215; Hill Country (Central Texas), 12, 81, 98, 99, 105; Piney Woods, 7, 43, 45, 110; Rolling Plains, 203; South Texas, 115, 129, 139, 161- 163, 174, 184; Trans-Pecos, 186, 188, 193, 199

Edinburg Scenic Wetlands, 159, 172
El Franco Lee Park, 15, 22
Elf Owls, 191
Ellen Trout Park, 43, 48
Endangered Species, 87, 98, 99, **135, 146, 156**; Endangered Species Act, **158**; habitat conservation, 19, 70, 99, 157
European Starlings, 4, 65

Ferruginous Hawks, 207, 211
festivals: Balcones Songbird Festival, 99; Hummingbird Festival, 147; Sparrowfest, 99; Whooping Crane Festival, 153
Field Sparrows, 63, 107, 120, 134, 213
flyways: Central Flyway, ix, 7, **9**, 38, 141, 188; Mississippi Flyway, ix, 7, **9**, 37, 50, 141; Pacific Flyway, **9**, 188
Fort Clark Springs, 113, 131
Fort Davis, Texas, 193, 195
Fort Worth Nature Center and Refuge, 56, 73
Forster's Terns, 37, 92, 210
Fox Sparrows, 48, 63, 75, 213
Franklin's Gulls, 92, 210
Fulvous Whistling Ducks, 35, 172

Gadwalls, 18, 48, 96, 131, 217; feather fact, **218**
Gage Hotel and Gardens, 186, 189
Galveston, Texas, 15, 17, 24–26
Galveston Bay, 29
Gambel's Quail, 213
Globally Important Bird Area, 31
Golden Eagles, 191, 211
Golden-cheeked Warblers, 3, 98, 105, 122, 134; feather fact, **100**
Golden-crowned Kinglets, 97, 120
Golden-fronted Woodpeckers, 118, 175, 181
Gonzalez, Karina, xi
Government Canyon State Natural Area, 122
Granger Lake, 79, 92; dam, 92; parks 92–93
Grasshopper Sparrows, 18, 167
Gray Catbirds, **44**, 50, 164
Gray Hawks, 181, 184, 192
Gray-cheeked Thrushes, 20, 33, 164
Great Blue Herons, 34, 48, 126, 139, 183, 212; feather fact, **95**; resident bird, 69, 116, 82, 162; rookery, 34, 153
Great Crested Flycatchers, 59, 69, 98, 116, 173